DISASTERS IN HISTORY

Shackleton and the Lost Antarctic Expedition

by B. A. Hoena

illustrated by Dave Hoover
and Charles Barnett III

Consultant:

Robert Headland

Archivist and Curator

Scott Polar Research Institute

University of Cambridge, United Kingdom

Capstone *press*

Mankato, Minnesota

Graphic Library is published by Capstone Press,
1710 Roe Crest Drive, North Mankato, Minnesota 56003.
www.capstonepub.com

Library of Congress Cataloging-in-Publication Data
Hoena, B. A.
Shackleton and the lost Antarctic expedition / by B. A. Hoena; illustrated by Dave Hoover and Charles Barnett III.
p. cm.—(Graphic library. Disasters in history)
Includes bibliographical references.
ISBN-13: 978-0-7368-5482-5 (hardcover)
ISBN-10: 0-7368-5482-7 (hardcover)
ISBN-13: 978-0-7368-6877-8 (softcover pbk.)
ISBN-10: 0-7368-6877-1 (softcover pbk.)
1. Shackleton, Ernest Henry, Sir, 1874–1922—Travel—Antarctica—Juvenile literature. 2. Imperial Trans-Antarctic Expedition (1914–1917)—Juvenile literature. 3. Antarctica—Discovery and exploration—British—Juvenile literature. 4. Endurance (Ship)—Juvenile literature. I. Hoover, Dave, 1955– ill. II. Barnett, Charles, III, ill. III. Title. IV. Series.
G850 1914 .S53 H63 2006
919.8'904—dc22 2005029848

Summary: In graphic novel format, tells the story of Antarctic explorer Ernest Shackleton and his failed attempt to cross the coldest and windiest continent on earth.

Art Direction and Design
Jason Knudson

Storyboard Artist
B. A. Hoena

Production Designer
Alison Thiele

Colorist
Benjamin Hunzeker

Editor
Erika L. Shores

Editor's note: Direct quotations from primary sources are indicated by a yellow background.

Direct quotations appear on the following pages:
Pages 6, 10, from crewmembers' diaries as quoted in *Endurance: Shackleton's Incredible Voyage* by Alfred Lansing, (Wheaton, Ill.: Tyndale House, 1999).
Pages 12, 15 (bottom), 21, from crewmembers' diaries and letters as quoted in *The* Endurance*: Shackleton's Legendary Antarctic Expedition* by Caroline Alexander, (New York: Alfred E. Knopf, 1998).
Pages 15 (top), 26, 27, from *South: A Memoir of the* Endurance *Voyage* by Ernest Shackleton, (New York: Carroll & Graf, 1998).

Printed in the United States 5946

Table of Contents

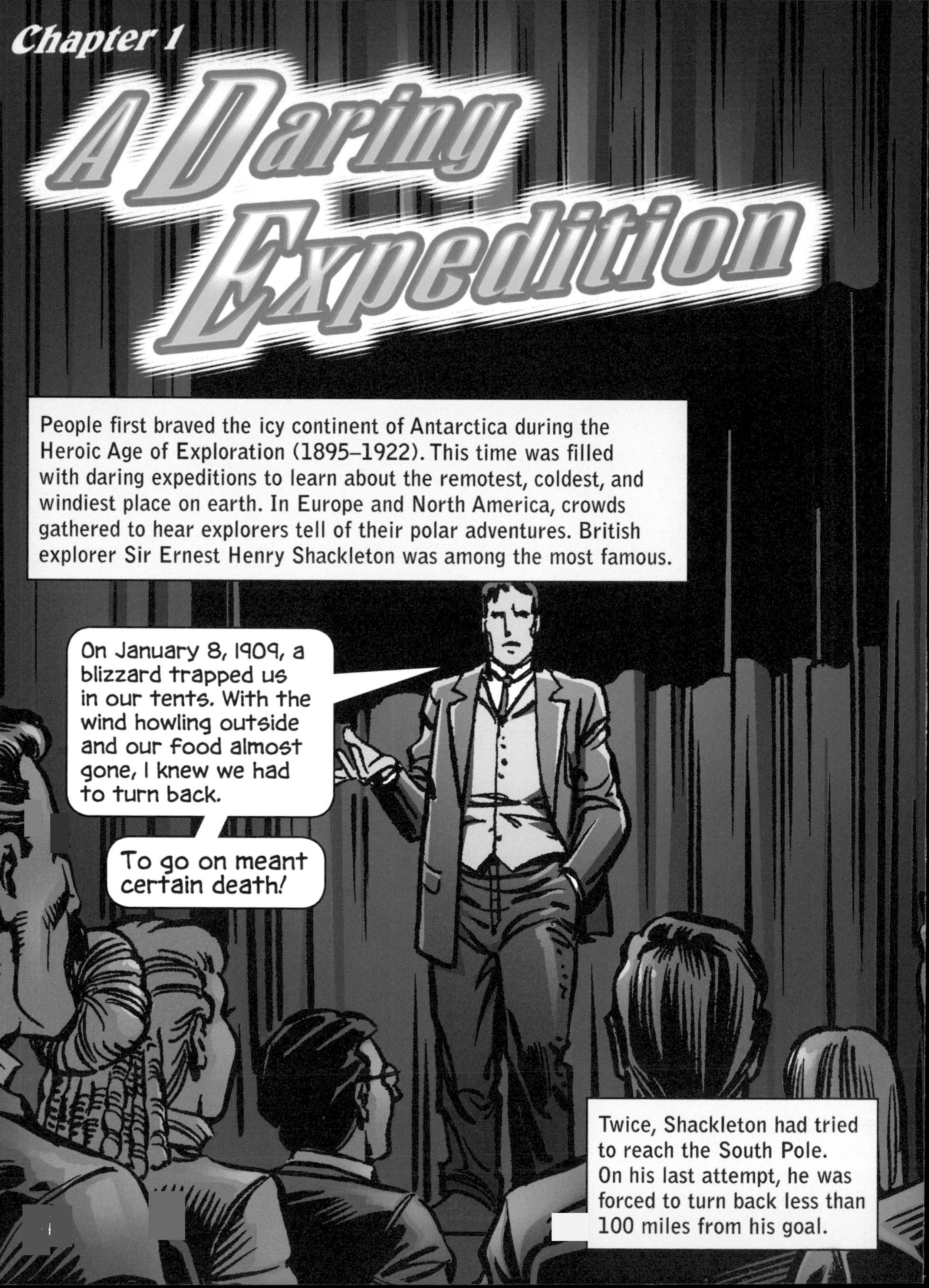
Chapter 1
A Daring Expedition
People first braved the icy continent of Antarctica during the Heroic Age of Exploration (1895–1922). This time was filled with daring expeditions to learn about the remotest, coldest, and windiest place on earth. In Europe and North America, crowds gathered to hear explorers tell of their polar adventures. British explorer Sir Ernest Henry Shackleton was among the most famous.
On January 8, 1909, a blizzard trapped us in our tents. With the wind howling outside and our food almost gone, I knew we had to turn back.
To go on meant certain death!
Twice, Shackleton had tried to reach the South Pole. On his last attempt, he was forced to turn back less than 100 miles from his goal.

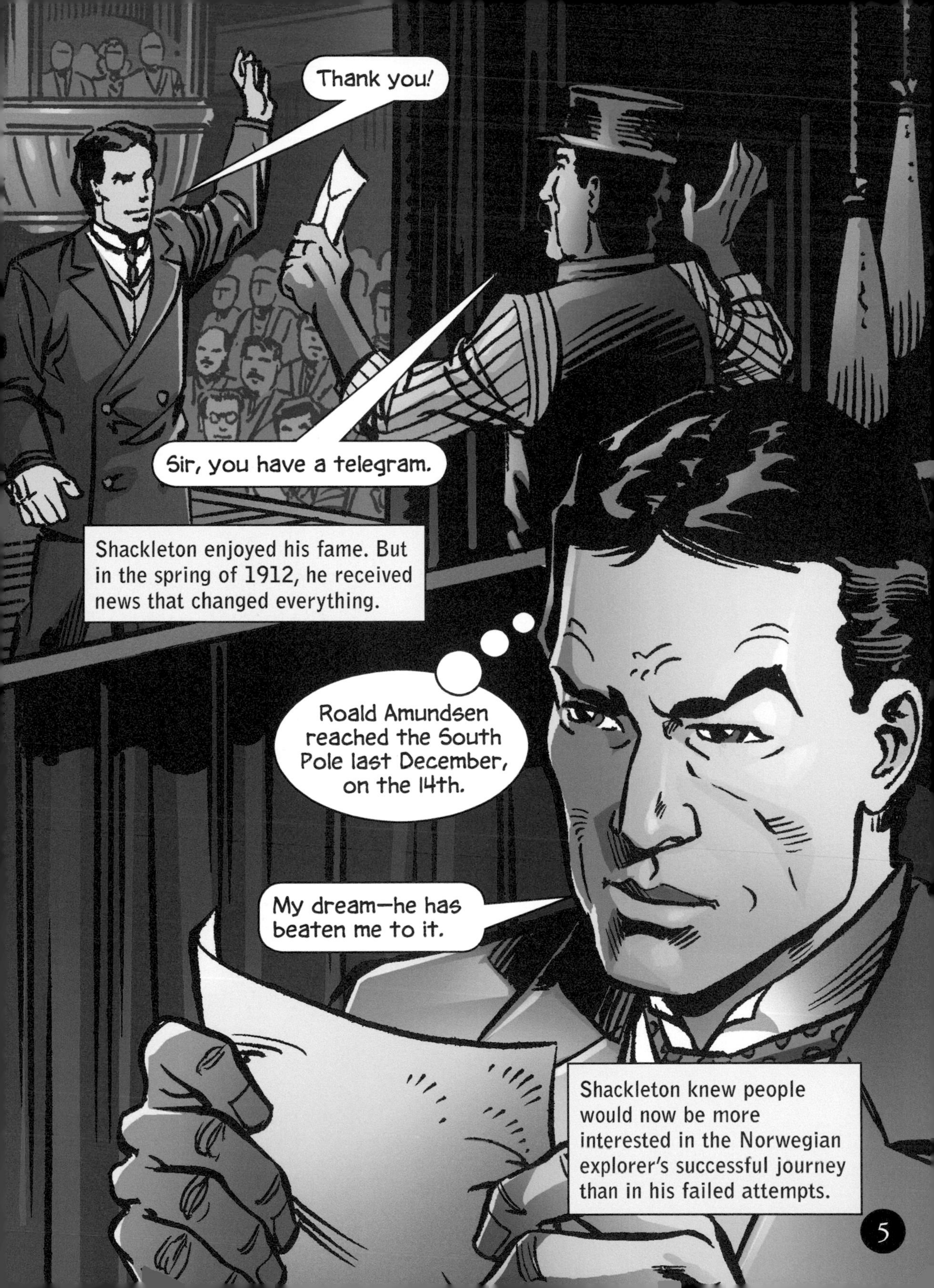
Thank you!
Sir, you have a telegram.
Shackleton enjoyed his fame. But in the spring of 1912, he received news that changed everything.
Roald Amundsen reached the South Pole last December, on the 14th.
My dream—he has beaten me to it.
Shackleton knew people would now be more interested in the Norwegian explorer's successful journey than in his failed attempts.

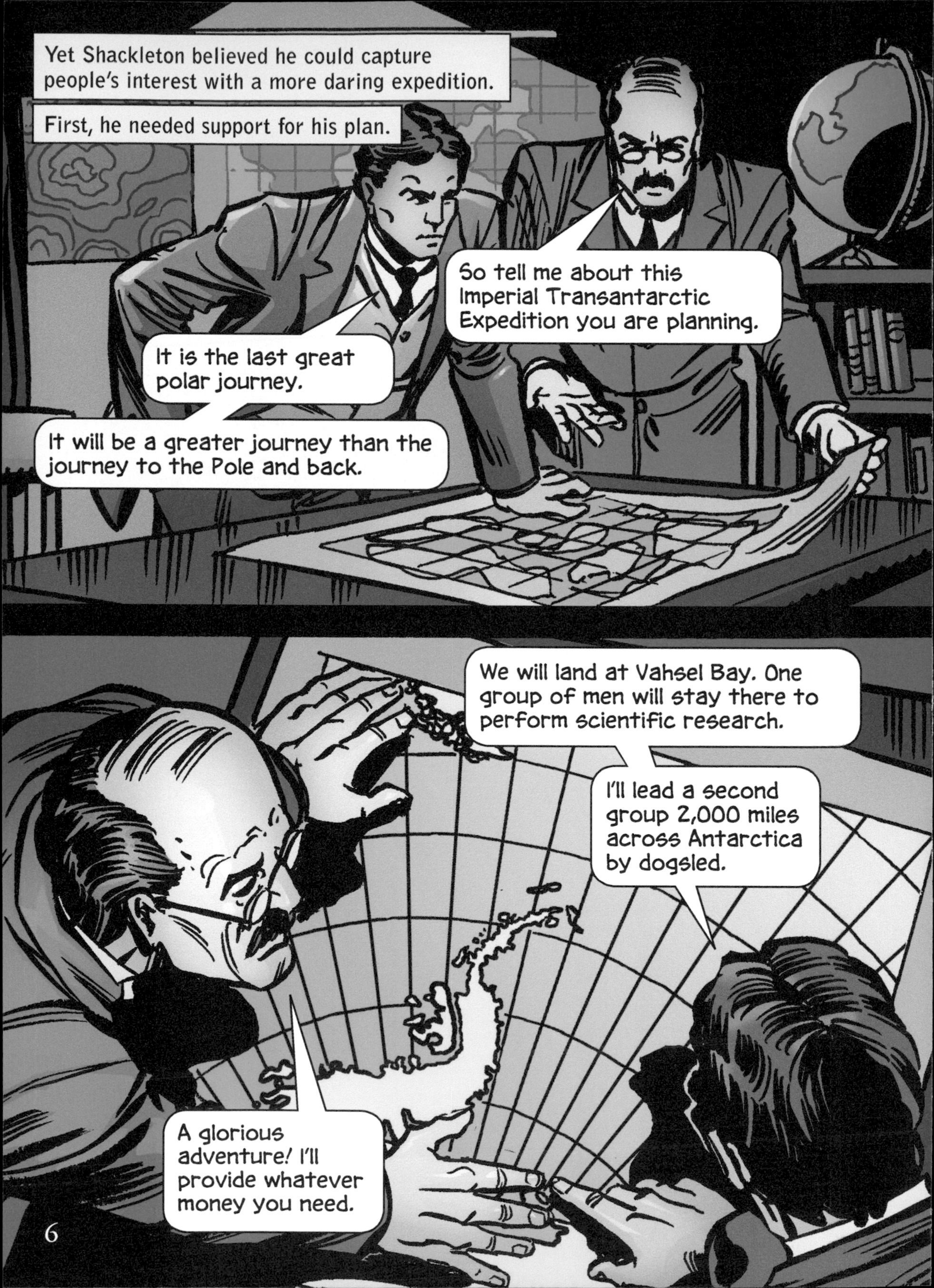
Yet Shackleton believed he could capture people's interest with a more daring expedition.
First, he needed support for his plan.
So tell me about this Imperial Transantarctic Expedition you are planning.
It is the last great polar journey.
It will be a greater journey than the journey to the Pole and back.
We will land at Vahsel Bay. One group of men will stay there to perform scientific research.
I'll lead a second group 2,000 miles across Antarctica by dogsled.
A glorious adventure! I'll provide whatever money you need.

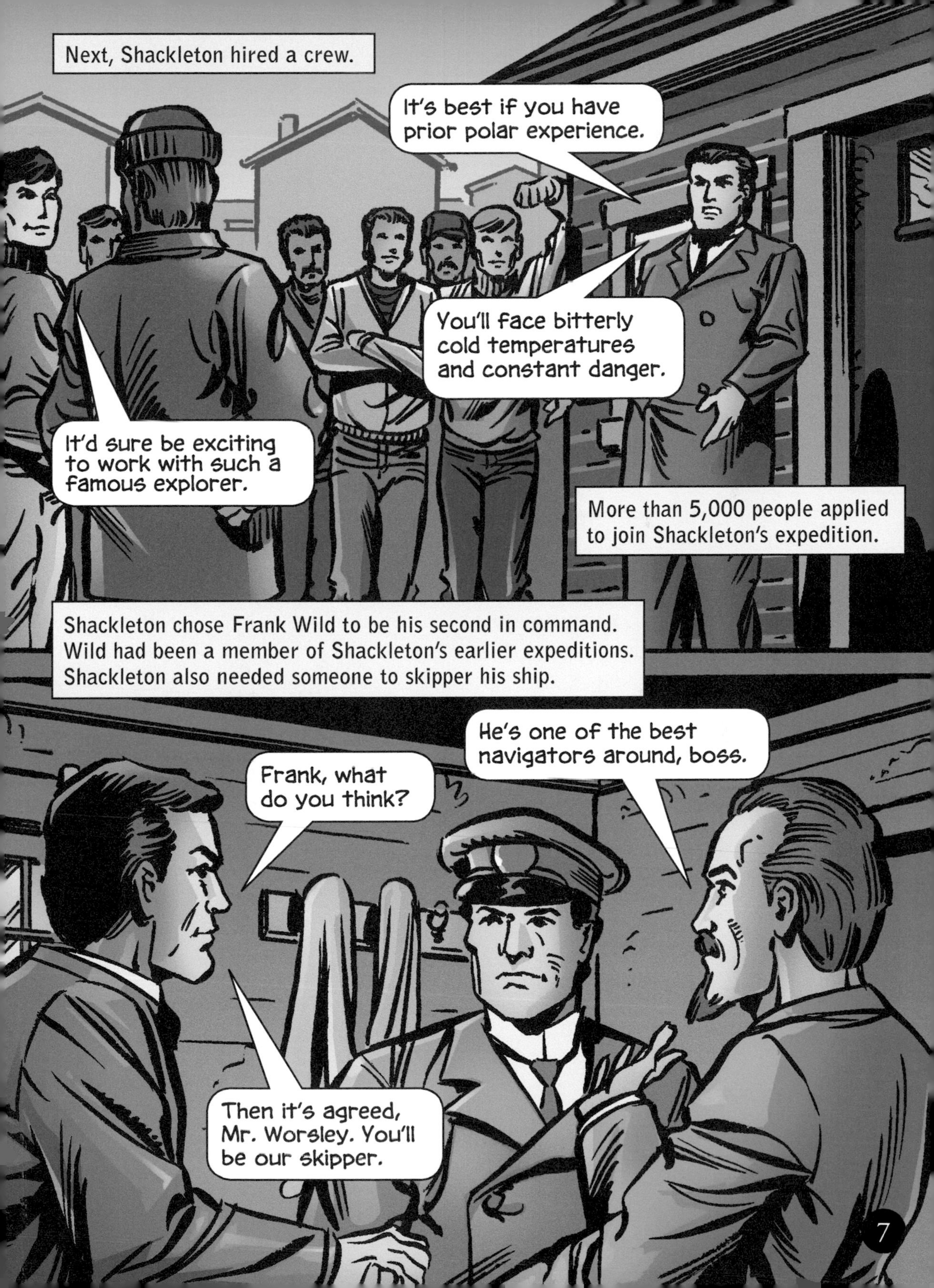
Next, Shackleton hired a crew.
It's best if you have prior polar experience.
You'll face bitterly cold temperatures and constant danger.
It'd sure be exciting to work with such a famous explorer.
More than 5,000 people applied to join Shackleton's expedition.
Shackleton chose Frank Wild to be his second in command. Wild had been a member of Shackleton's earlier expeditions. Shackleton also needed someone to skipper his ship.
Frank, what do you think?
He's one of the best navigators around, boss.
Then it's agreed, Mr. Worsley. You'll be our skipper.

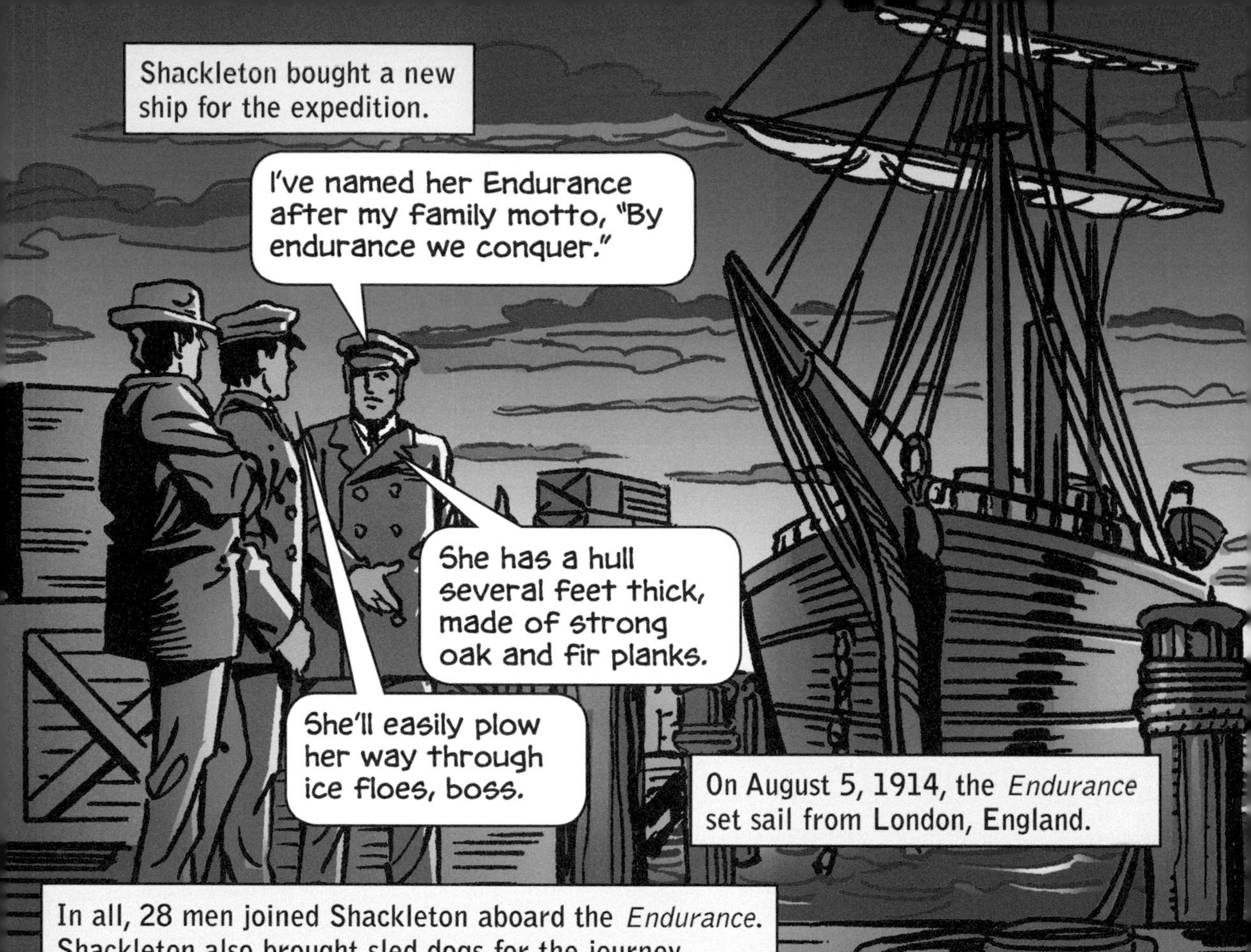

Shackleton bought a new ship for the expedition.
I've named her Endurance after my family motto, "By endurance we conquer."
She has a hull several feet thick, made of strong oak and fir planks.
She'll easily plow her way through ice floes, boss.
On August 5, 1914, the *Endurance* set sail from London, England.

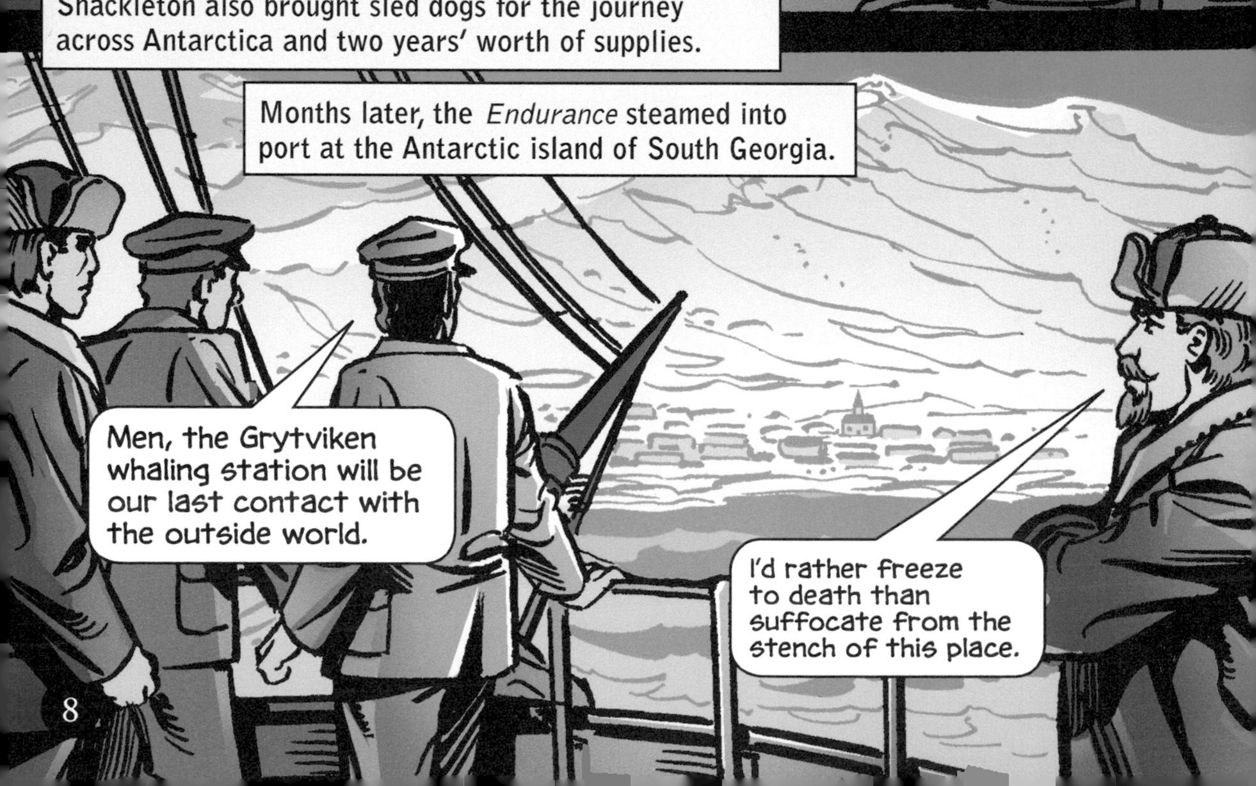

In all, 28 men joined Shackleton aboard the *Endurance*. Shackleton also brought sled dogs for the journey across Antarctica and two years' worth of supplies.
Months later, the *Endurance* steamed into port at the Antarctic island of South Georgia.
Men, the Grytviken whaling station will be our last contact with the outside world.
I'd rather freeze to death than suffocate from the stench of this place.

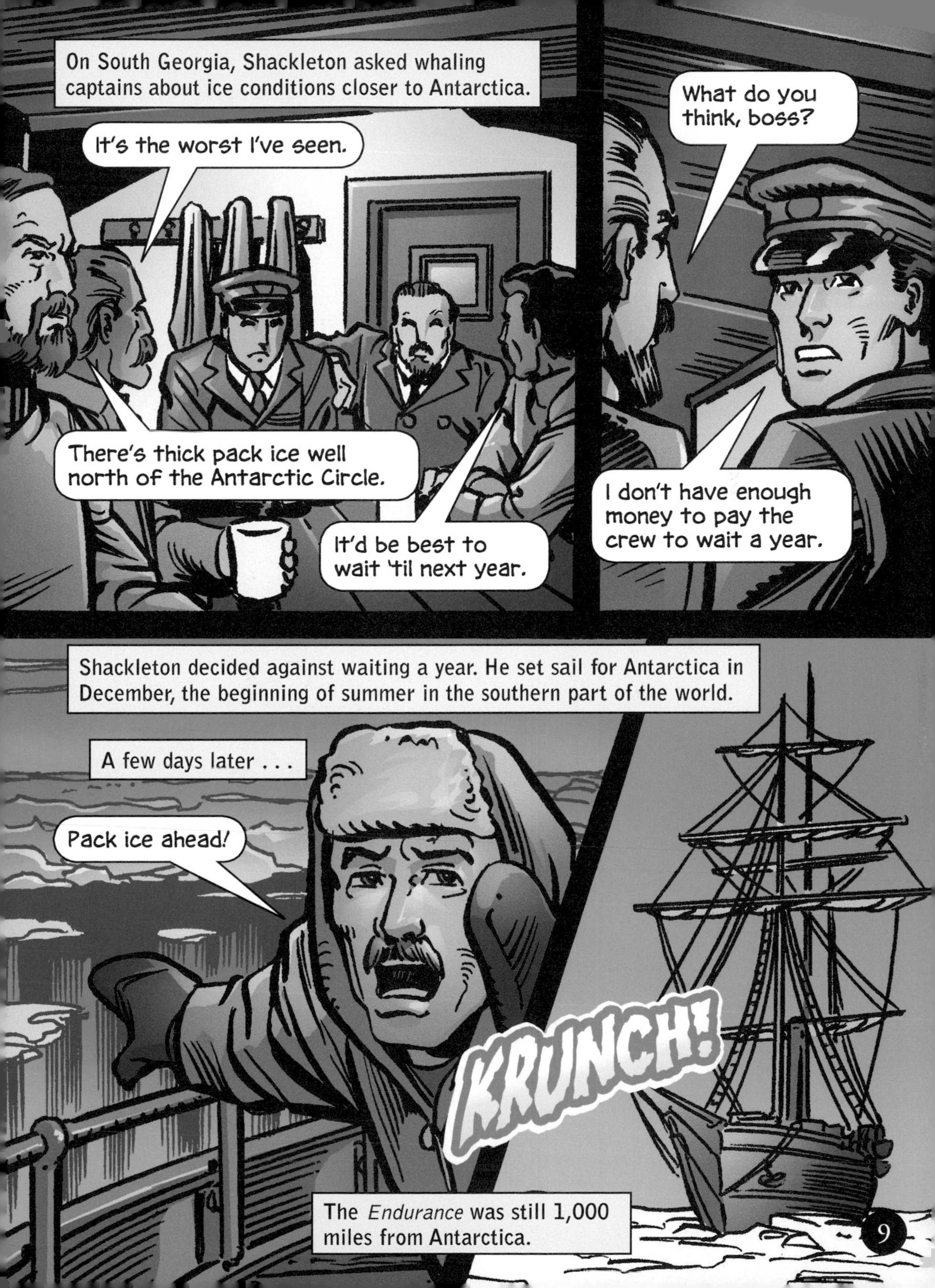
On South Georgia, Shackleton asked whaling captains about ice conditions closer to Antarctica.
It's the worst I've seen.
There's thick pack ice well north of the Antarctic Circle.
It'd be best to wait 'til next year.
What do you think, boss?
I don't have enough money to pay the crew to wait a year.
Shackleton decided against waiting a year. He set sail for Antarctica in December, the beginning of summer in the southern part of the world.
A few days later . . .
Pack ice ahead!
KRUNCH!
The *Endurance* was still 1,000 miles from Antarctica.

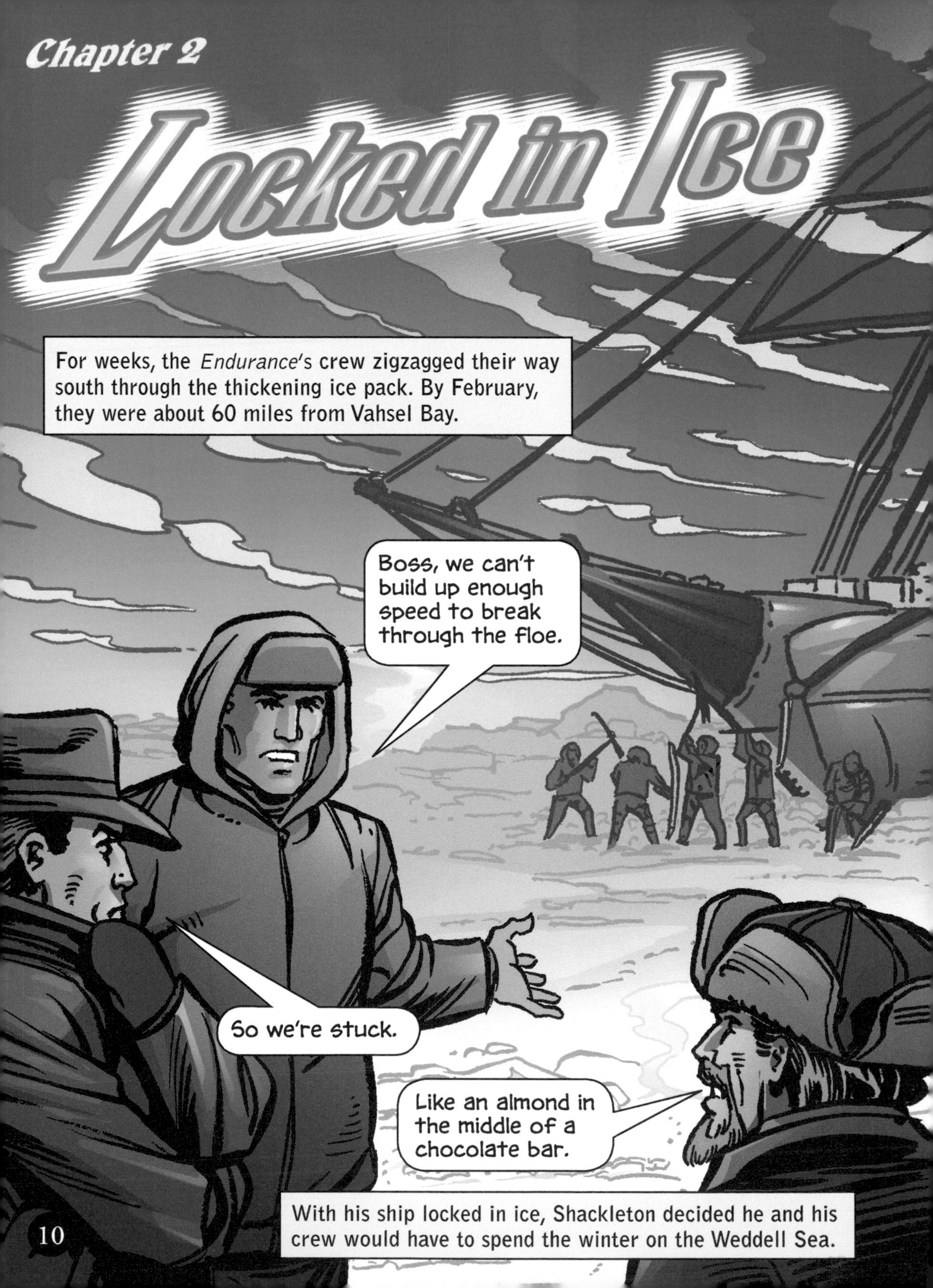
Chapter 2
Locked in Ice
For weeks, the *Endurance*'s crew zigzagged their way south through the thickening ice pack. By February, they were about 60 miles from Vahsel Bay.
Boss, we can't build up enough speed to break through the floe.
So we're stuck.
Like an almond in the middle of a chocolate bar.
With his ship locked in ice, Shackleton decided he and his crew would have to spend the winter on the Weddell Sea.

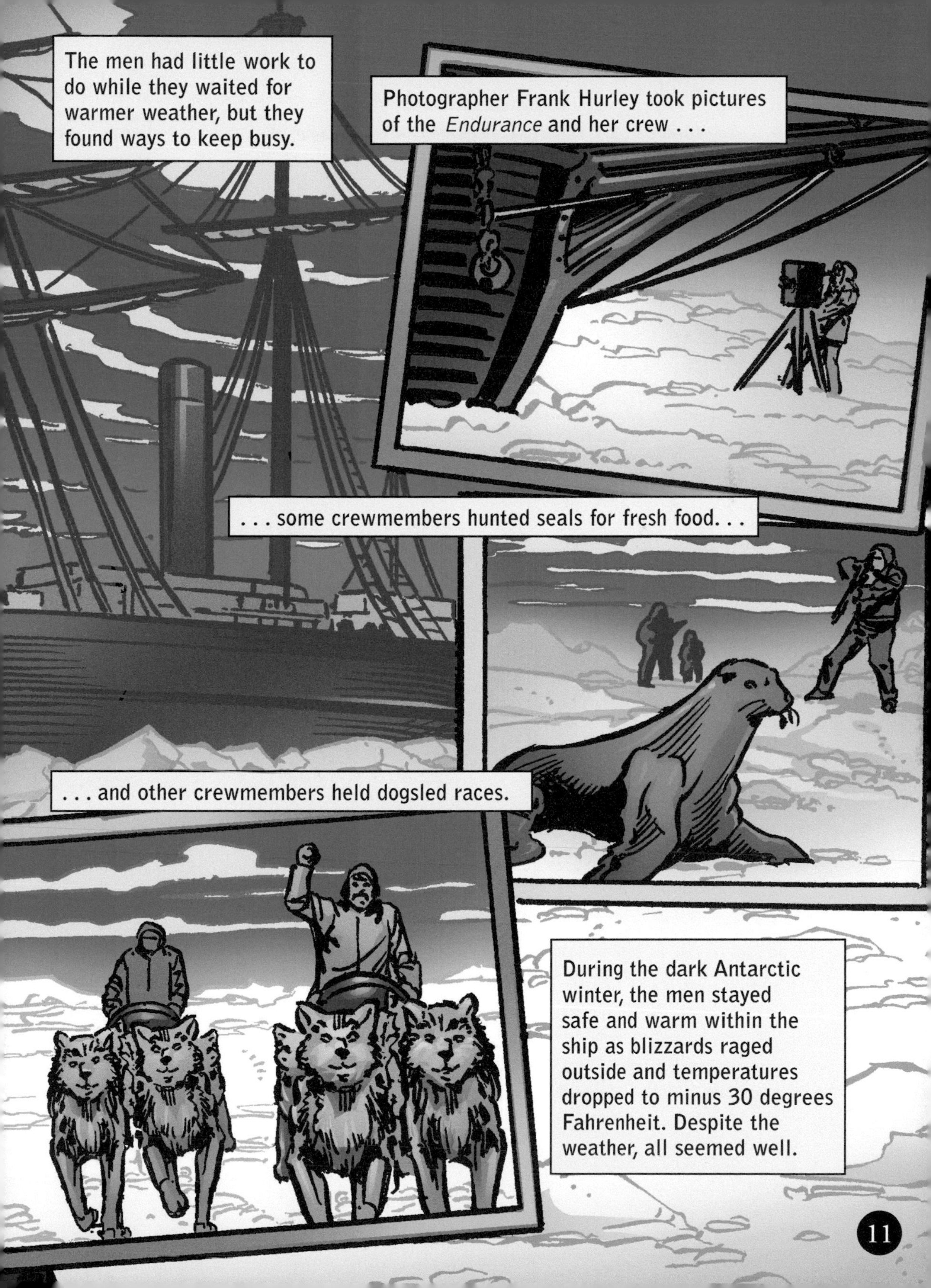
The men had little work to do while they waited for warmer weather, but they found ways to keep busy.
Photographer Frank Hurley took pictures of the *Endurance* and her crew . . .
. . . some crewmembers hunted seals for fresh food. . .
. . . and other crewmembers held dogsled races.
During the dark Antarctic winter, the men stayed safe and warm within the ship as blizzards raged outside and temperatures dropped to minus 30 degrees Fahrenheit. Despite the weather, all seemed well.

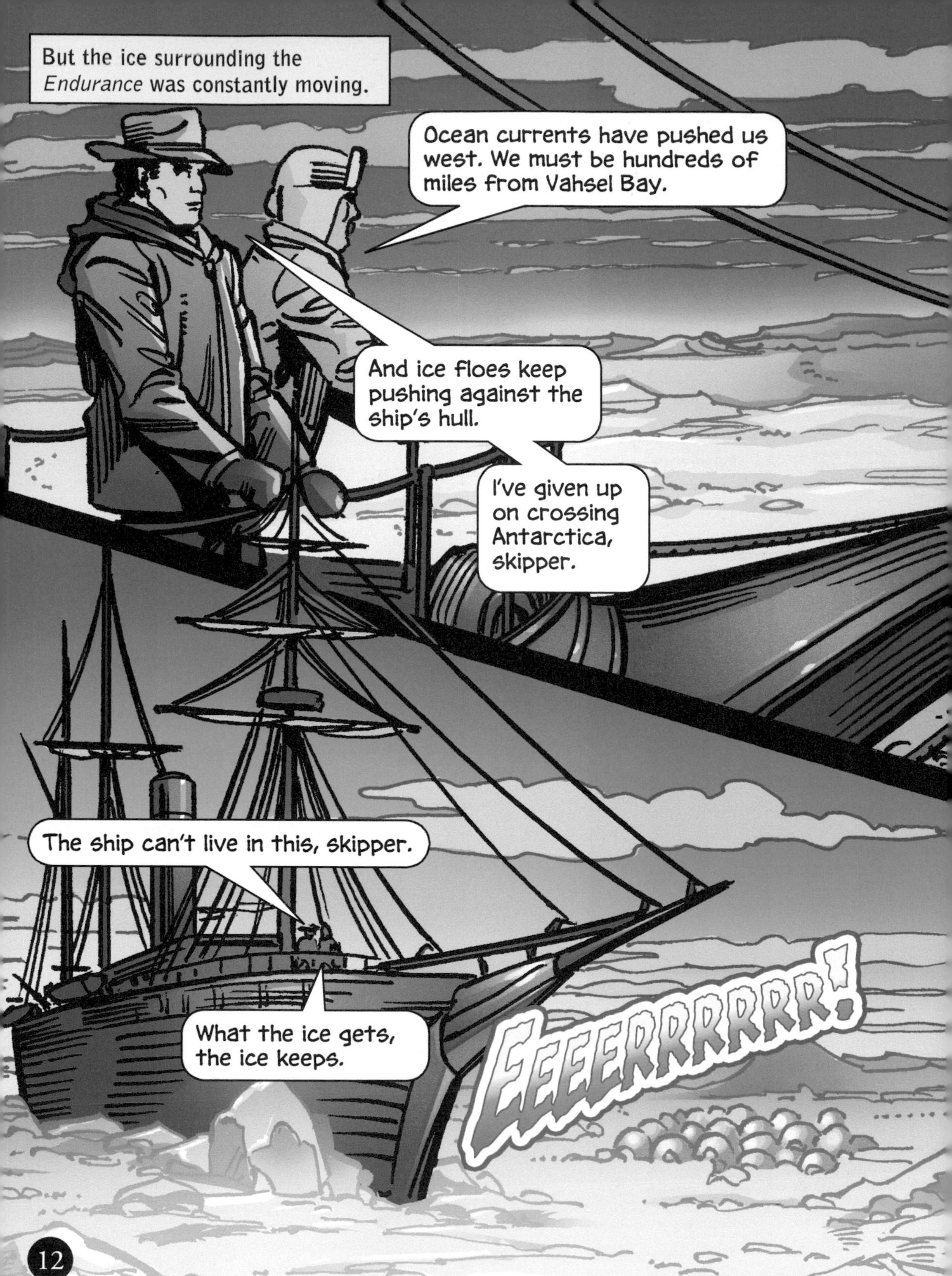

But the ice surrounding the *Endurance* was constantly moving.
Ocean currents have pushed us west. We must be hundreds of miles from Vahsel Bay.
And ice floes keep pushing against the ship's hull.
I've given up on crossing Antarctica, skipper.
The ship can't live in this, skipper.
What the ice gets, the ice keeps.
EEEERRRRRR!

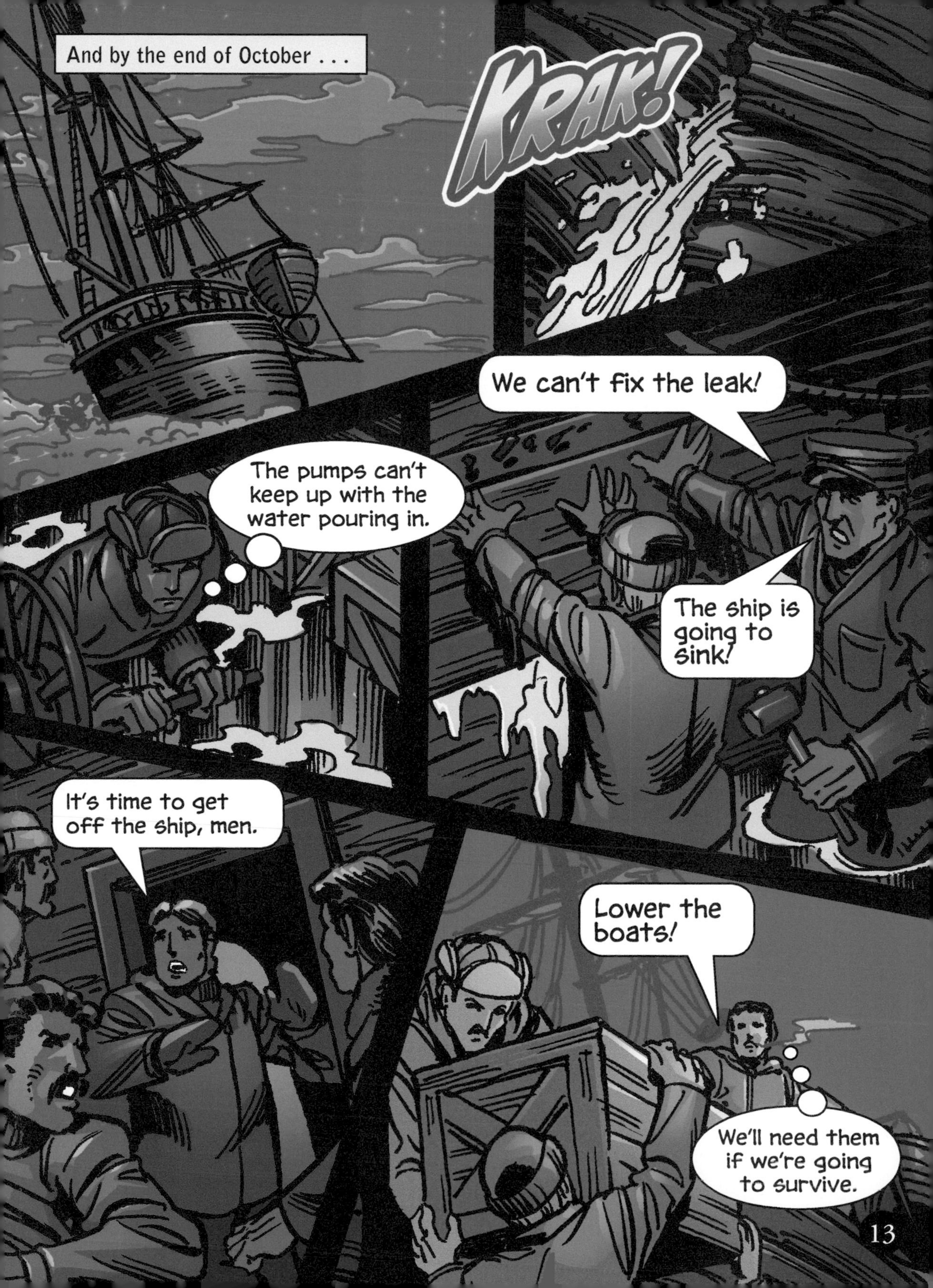
And by the end of October . . .
KRAK!
We can't fix the leak!
The ship is going to sink!
The pumps can't keep up with the water pouring in.
It's time to get off the ship, men.
Lower the boats!
We'll need them if we're going to survive.

Chapter 3
The Fight to Survive

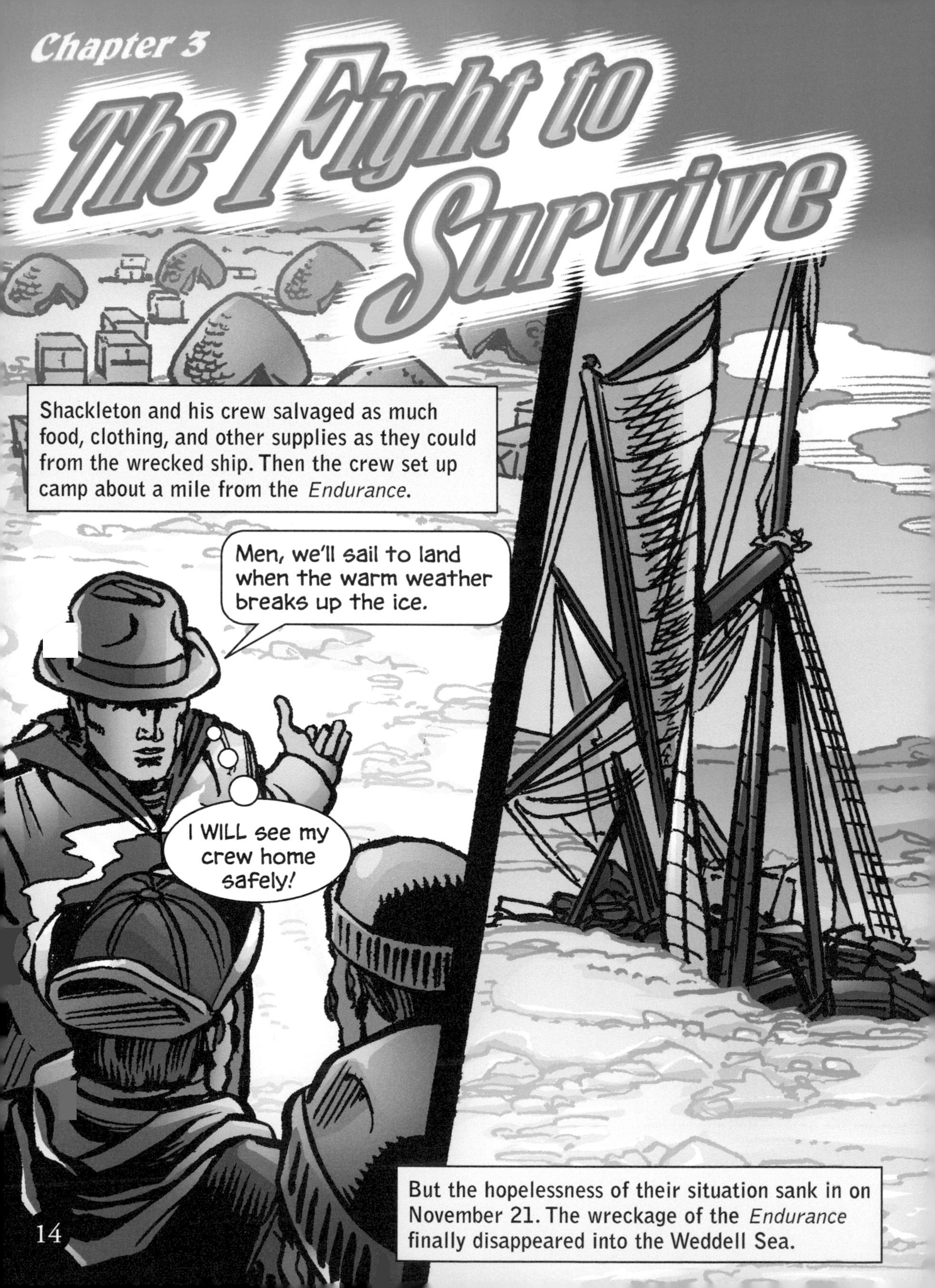

Shackleton and his crew salvaged as much food, clothing, and other supplies as they could from the wrecked ship. Then the crew set up camp about a mile from the *Endurance*.
Men, we'll sail to land when the warm weather breaks up the ice.
I WILL see my crew home safely!
But the hopelessness of their situation sank in on November 21. The wreckage of the *Endurance* finally disappeared into the Weddell Sea.

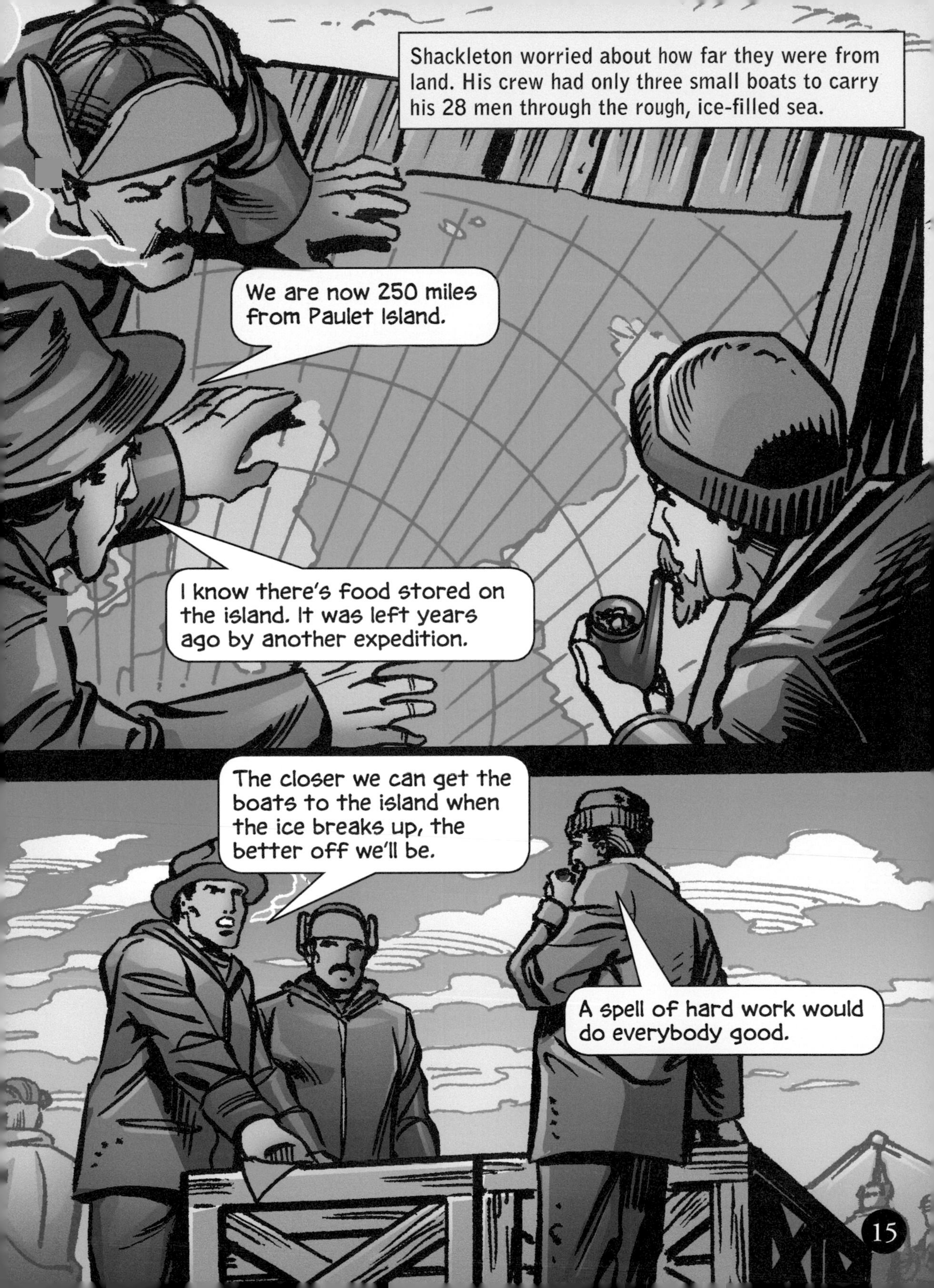
Shackleton worried about how far they were from land. His crew had only three small boats to carry his 28 men through the rough, ice-filled sea.
We are now 250 miles from Paulet Island.
I know there's food stored on the island. It was left years ago by another expedition.
The closer we can get the boats to the island when the ice breaks up, the better off we'll be.
A spell of hard work would do everybody good.

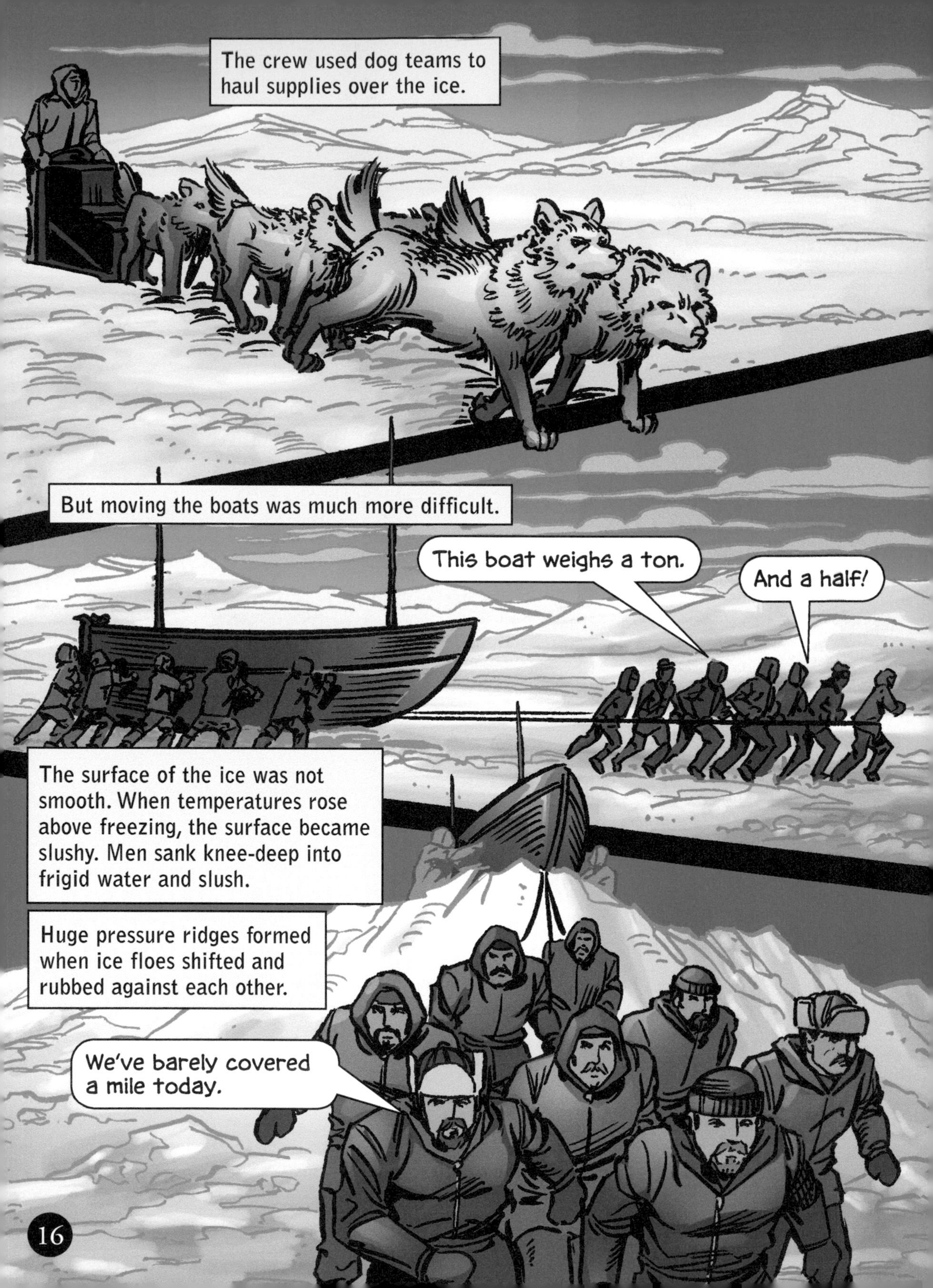
The crew used dog teams to haul supplies over the ice.
But moving the boats was much more difficult.
This boat weighs a ton.
And a half!
The surface of the ice was not smooth. When temperatures rose above freezing, the surface became slushy. Men sank knee-deep into frigid water and slush.
Huge pressure ridges formed when ice floes shifted and rubbed against each other.
We've barely covered a mile today.

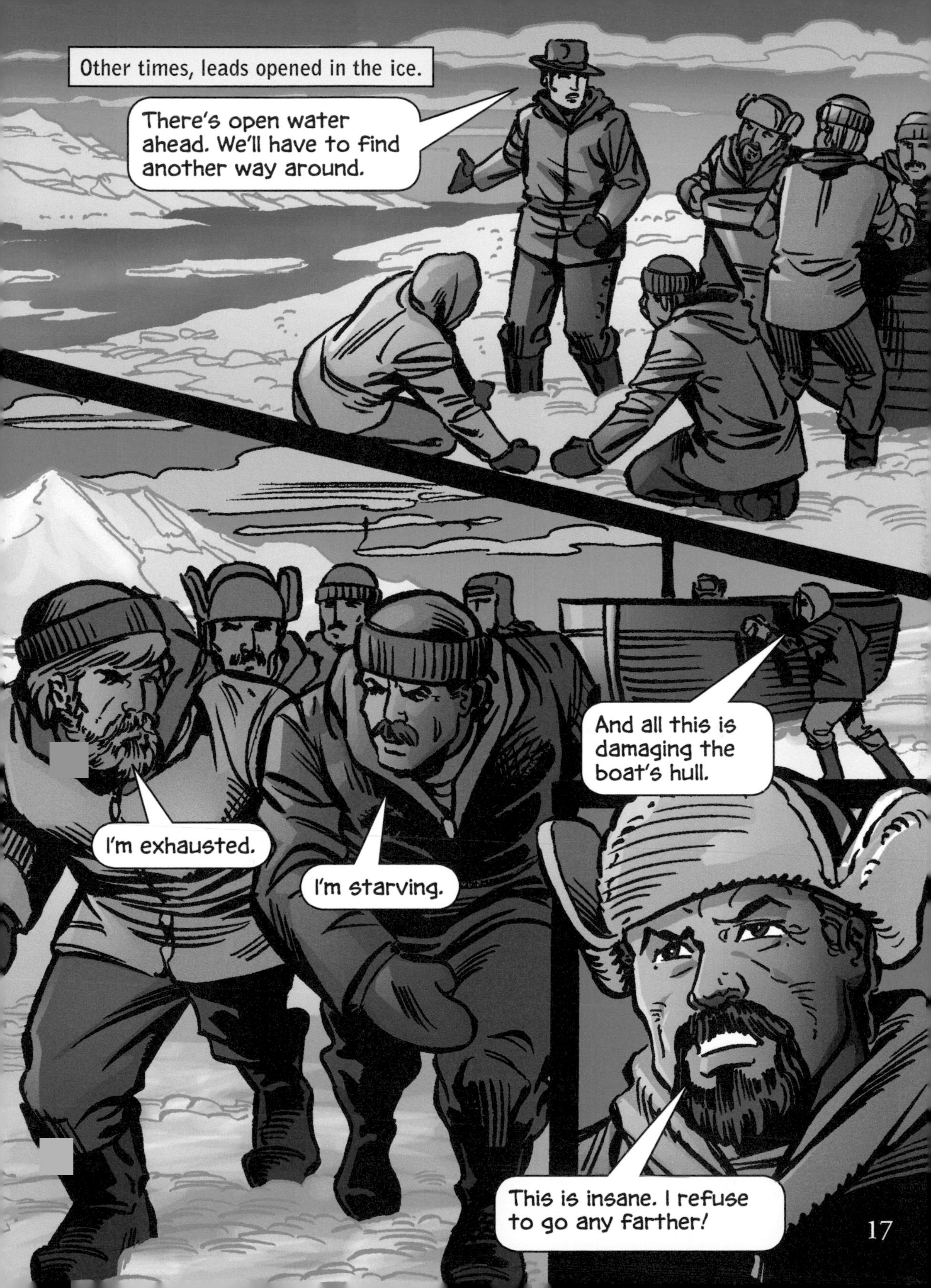
Other times, leads opened in the ice.
There's open water ahead. We'll have to find another way around.
I'm exhausted.
I'm starving.
And all this is damaging the boat's hull.
This is insane. I refuse to go any farther!

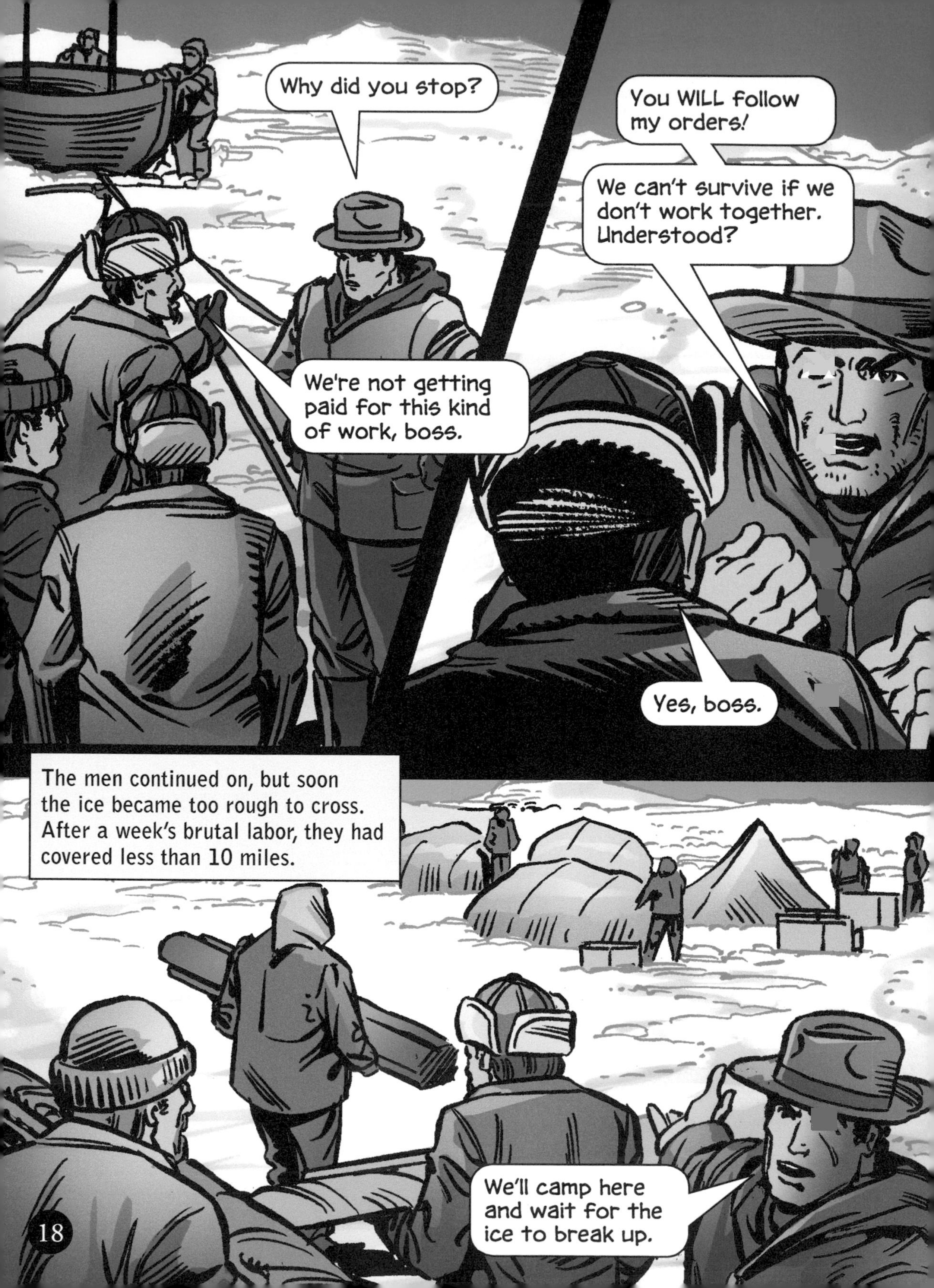
Why did you stop?
We're not getting paid for this kind of work, boss.
You WILL follow my orders!
We can't survive if we don't work together. Understood?
Yes, boss.
The men continued on, but soon the ice became too rough to cross. After a week's brutal labor, they had covered less than 10 miles.
We'll camp here and wait for the ice to break up.

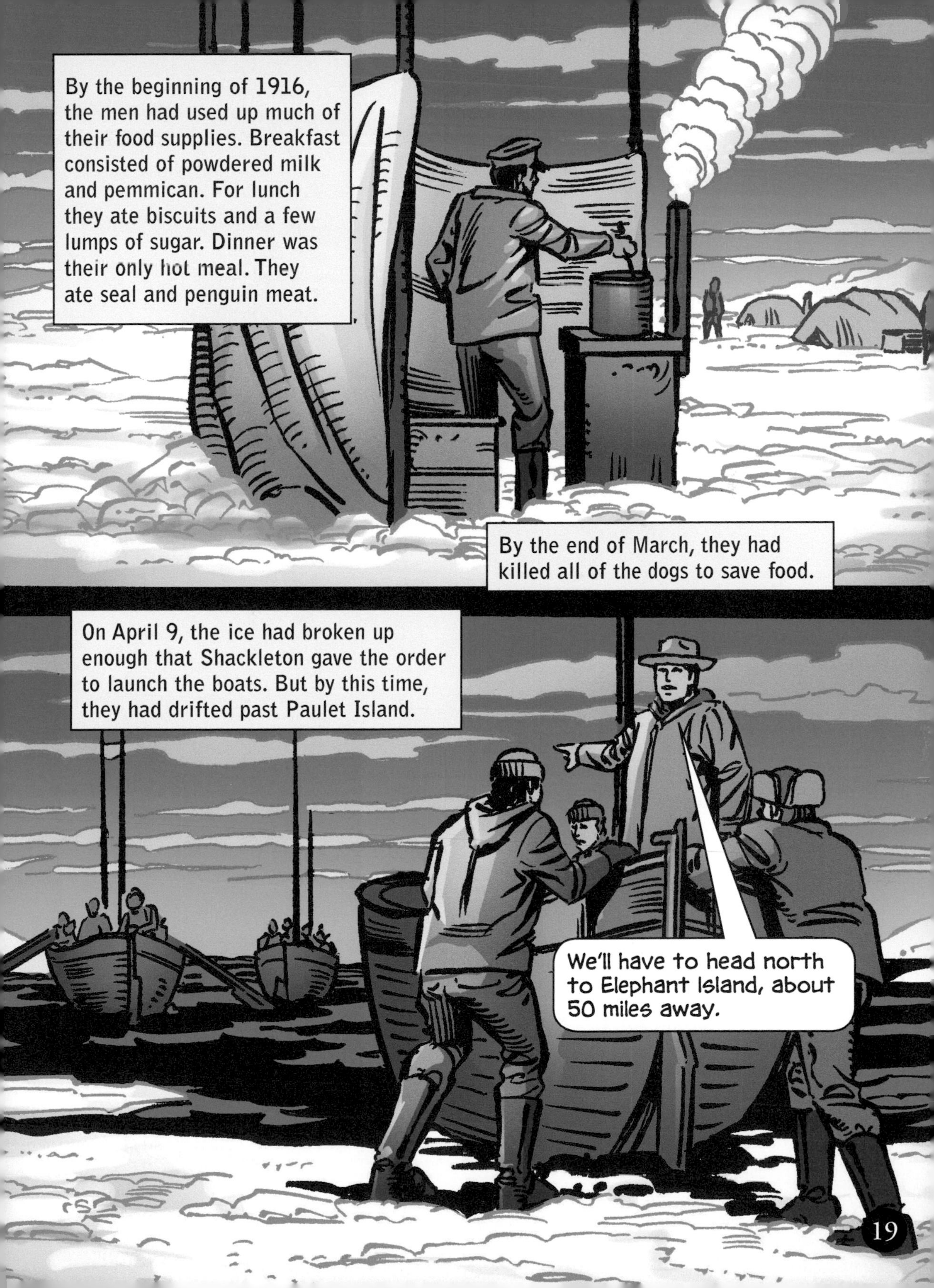
By the beginning of 1916, the men had used up much of their food supplies. Breakfast consisted of powdered milk and pemmican. For lunch they ate biscuits and a few lumps of sugar. Dinner was their only hot meal. They ate seal and penguin meat.
By the end of March, they had killed all of the dogs to save food.
On April 9, the ice had broken up enough that Shackleton gave the order to launch the boats. But by this time, they had drifted past Paulet Island.
We'll have to head north to Elephant Island, about 50 miles away.

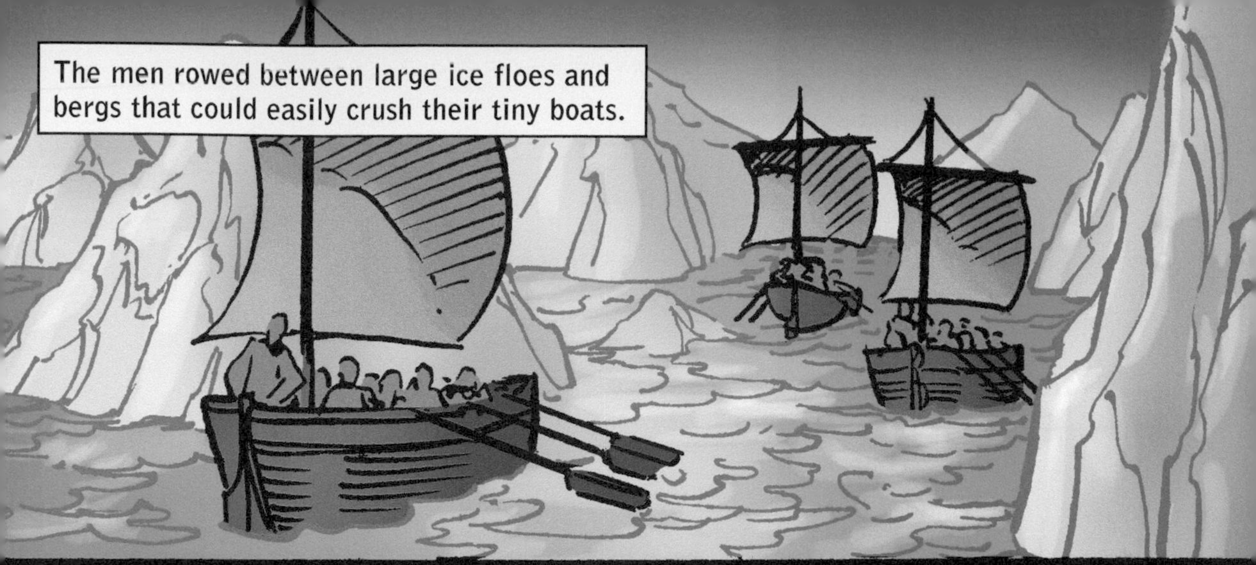
The men rowed between large ice floes and bergs that could easily crush their tiny boats.

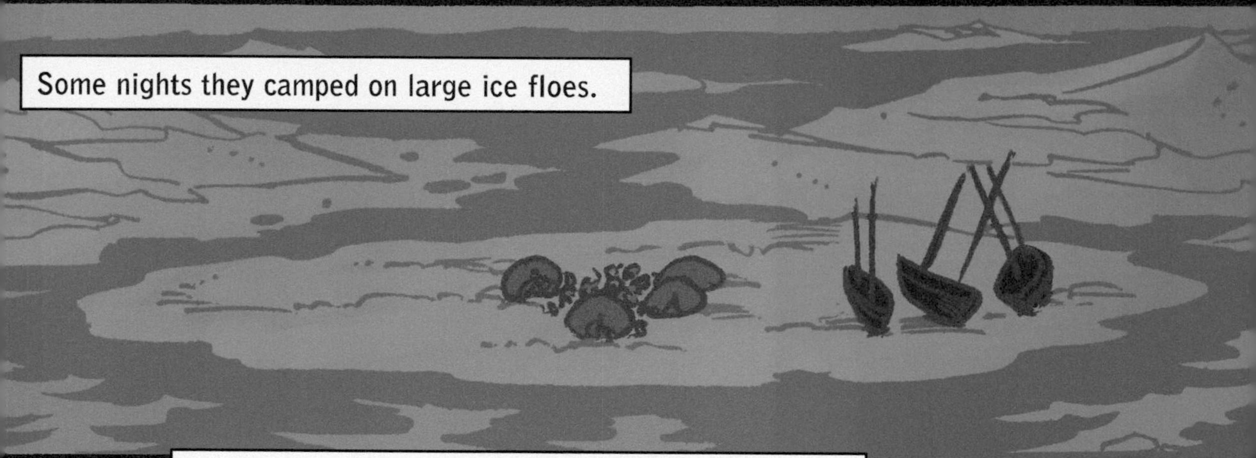
Some nights they camped on large ice floes.

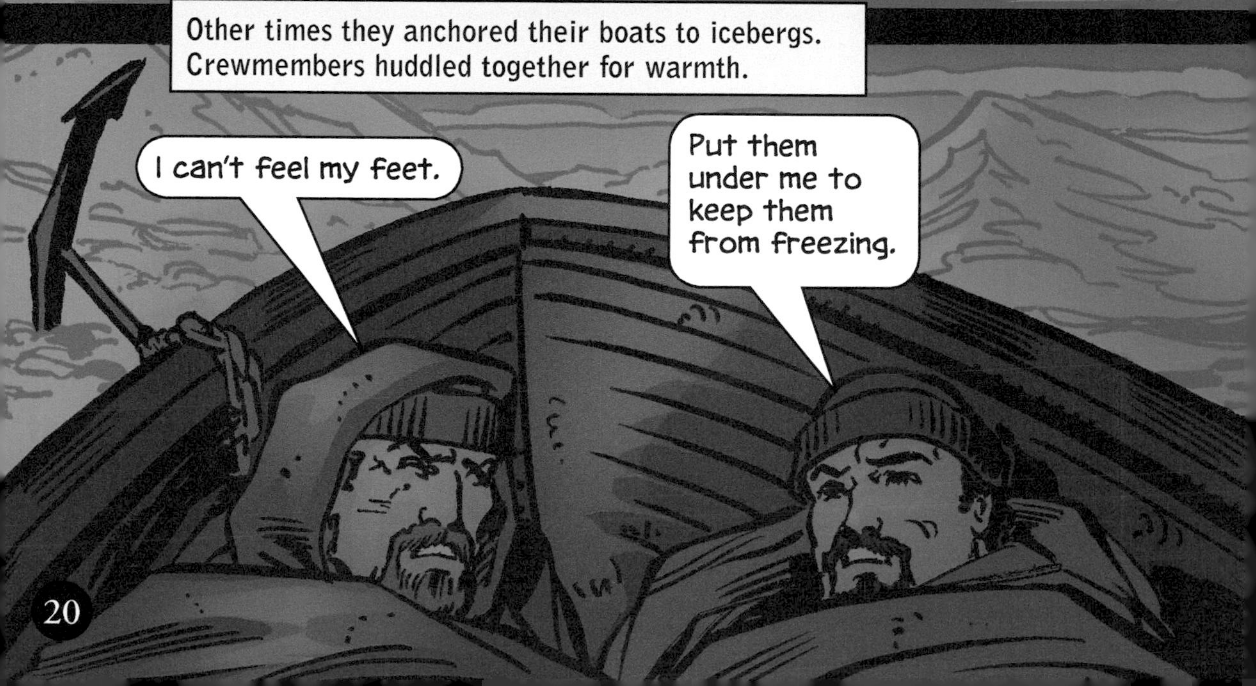
Other times they anchored their boats to icebergs. Crewmembers huddled together for warmth.
I can't feel my feet.
Put them under me to keep them from freezing.

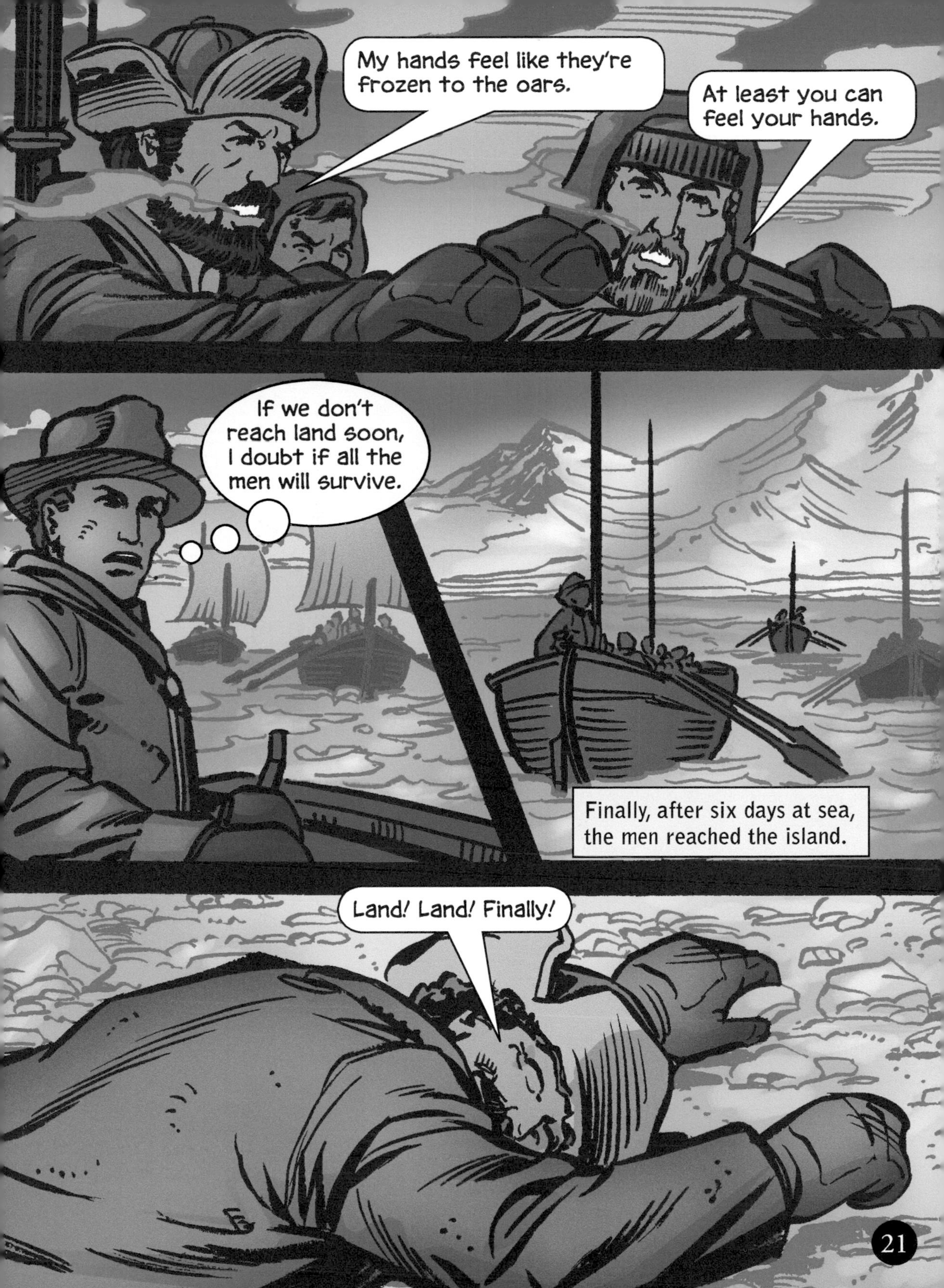
My hands feel like they're frozen to the oars.
At least you can feel your hands.
If we don't reach land soon, I doubt if all the men will survive.
Finally, after six days at sea, the men reached the island.
Land! Land! Finally!

Chapter 4

Rescue

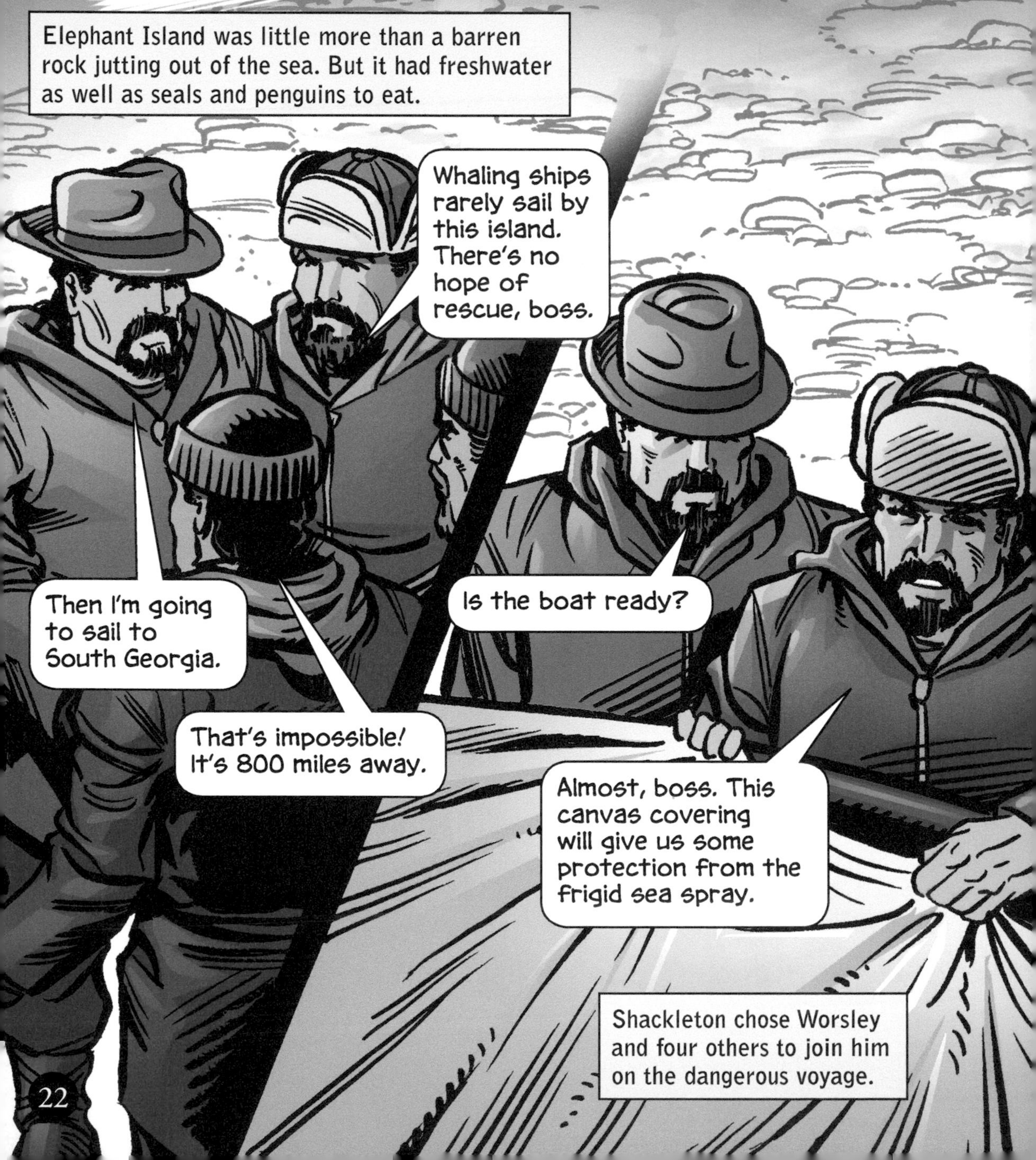

Elephant Island was little more than a barren rock jutting out of the sea. But it had freshwater as well as seals and penguins to eat.
Whaling ships rarely sail by this island. There's no hope of rescue, boss.
Then I'm going to sail to South Georgia.
That's impossible! It's 800 miles away.
Is the boat ready?
Almost, boss. This canvas covering will give us some protection from the frigid sea spray.
Shackleton chose Worsley and four others to join him on the dangerous voyage.

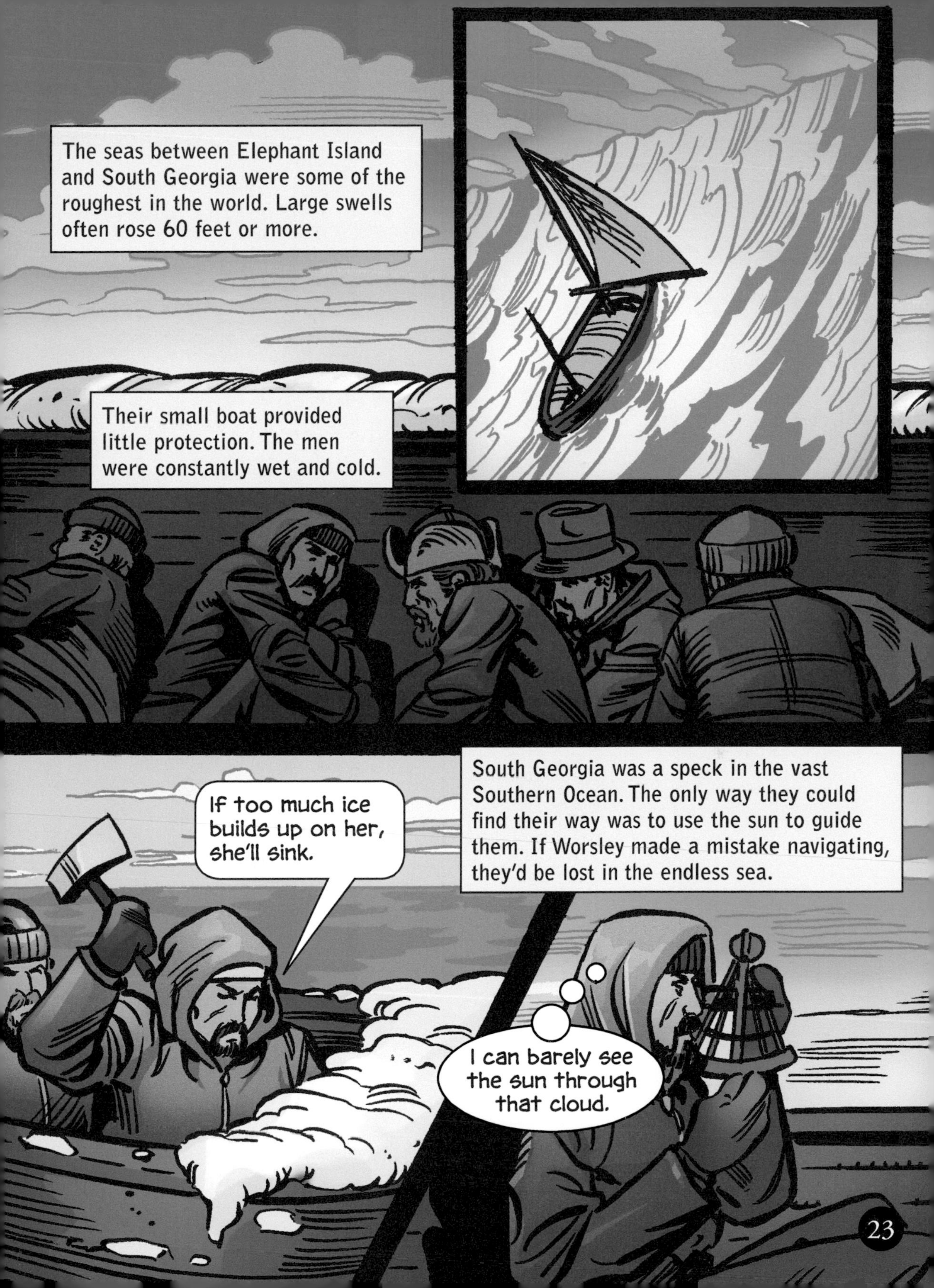
The seas between Elephant Island and South Georgia were some of the roughest in the world. Large swells often rose 60 feet or more.
Their small boat provided little protection. The men were constantly wet and cold.
If too much ice builds up on her, she'll sink.
South Georgia was a speck in the vast Southern Ocean. The only way they could find their way was to use the sun to guide them. If Worsley made a mistake navigating, they'd be lost in the endless sea.
I can barely see the sun through that cloud.

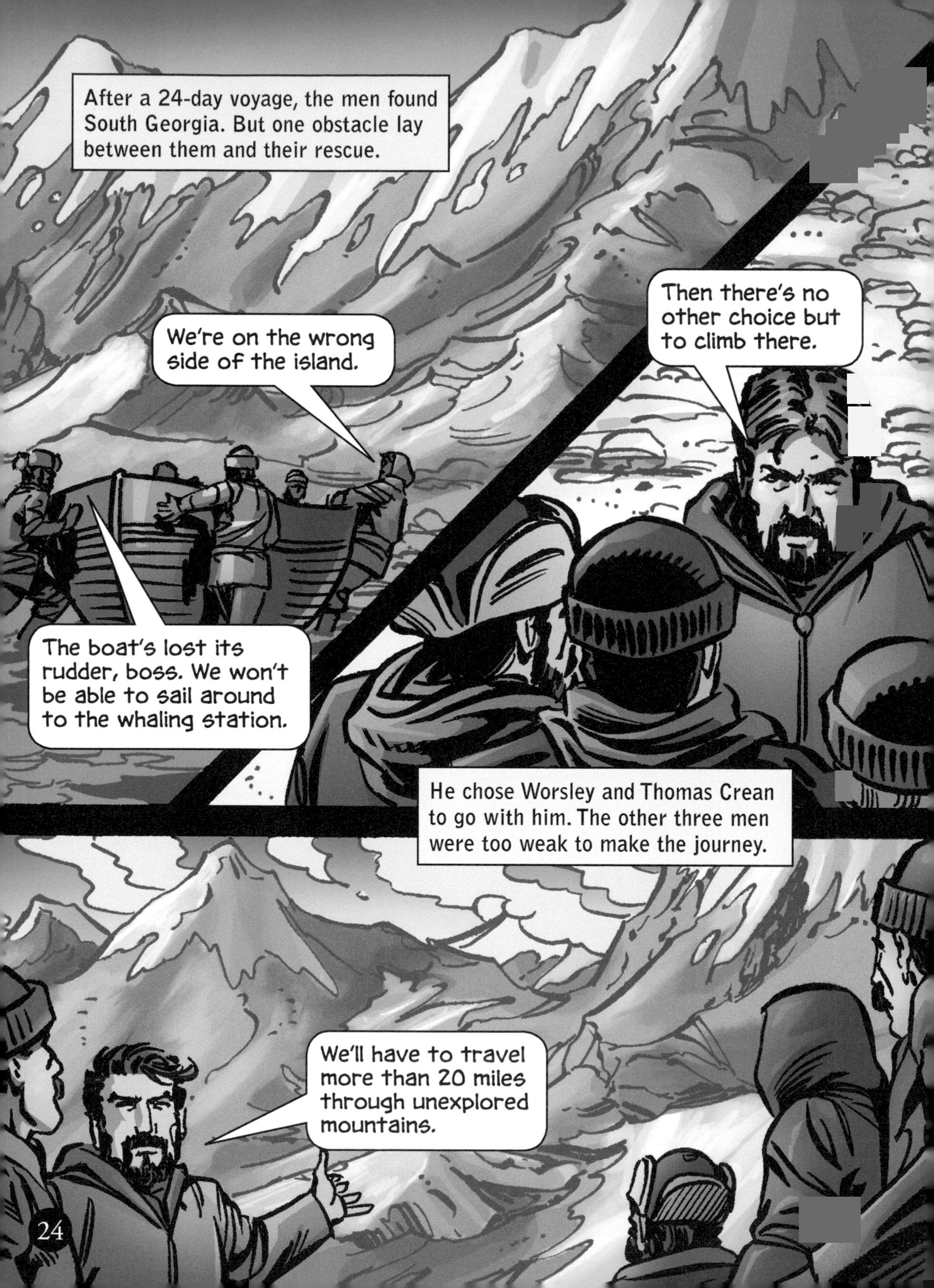
After a 24-day voyage, the men found South Georgia. But one obstacle lay between them and their rescue.
We're on the wrong side of the island.
The boat's lost its rudder, boss. We won't be able to sail around to the whaling station.
Then there's no other choice but to climb there.
He chose Worsley and Thomas Crean to go with him. The other three men were too weak to make the journey.
We'll have to travel more than 20 miles through unexplored mountains.

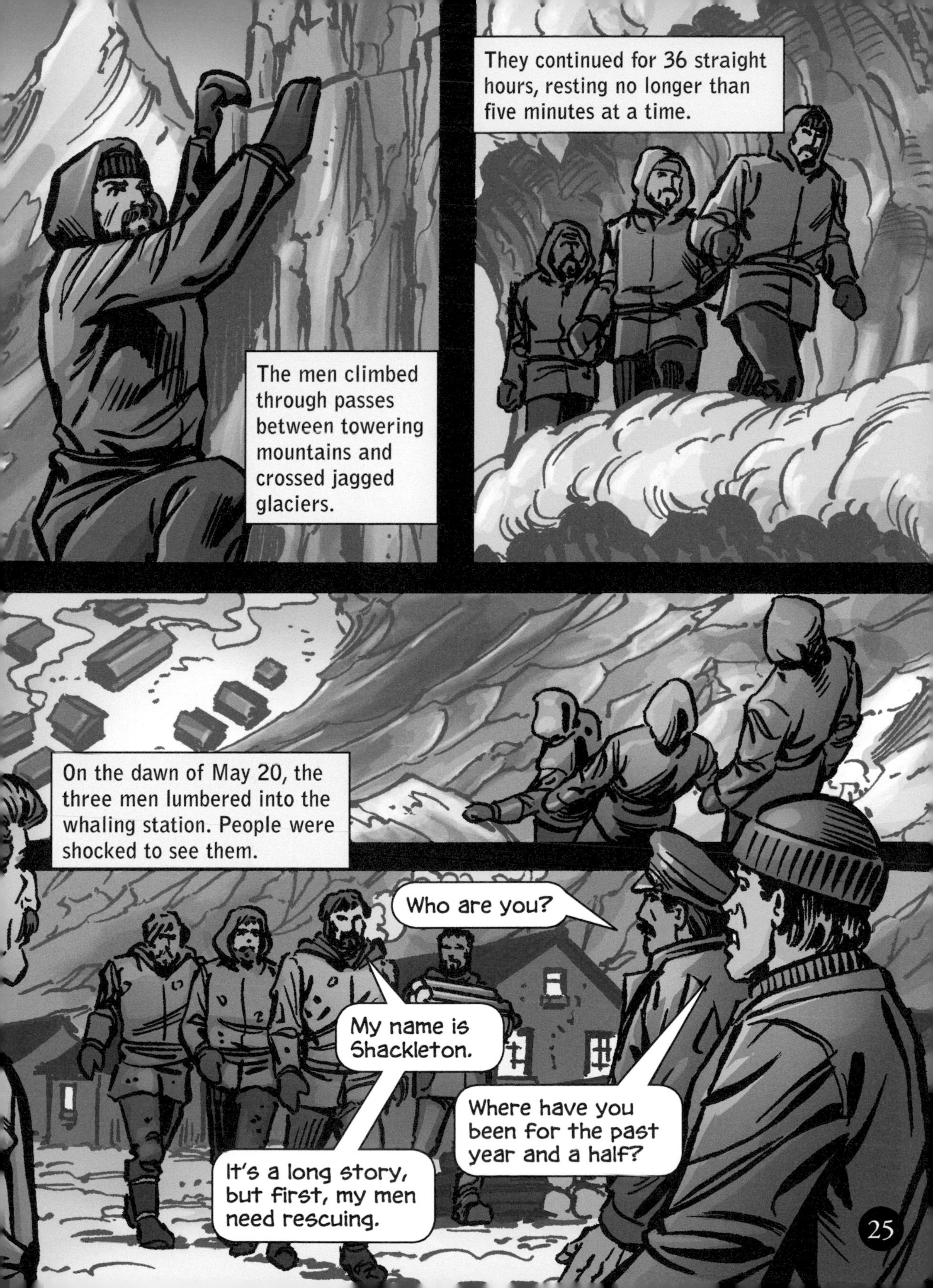
The men climbed through passes between towering mountains and crossed jagged glaciers.
They continued for 36 straight hours, resting no longer than five minutes at a time.
On the dawn of May 20, the three men lumbered into the whaling station. People were shocked to see them.
Who are you?
My name is Shackleton.
Where have you been for the past year and a half?
It's a long story, but first, my men need rescuing.

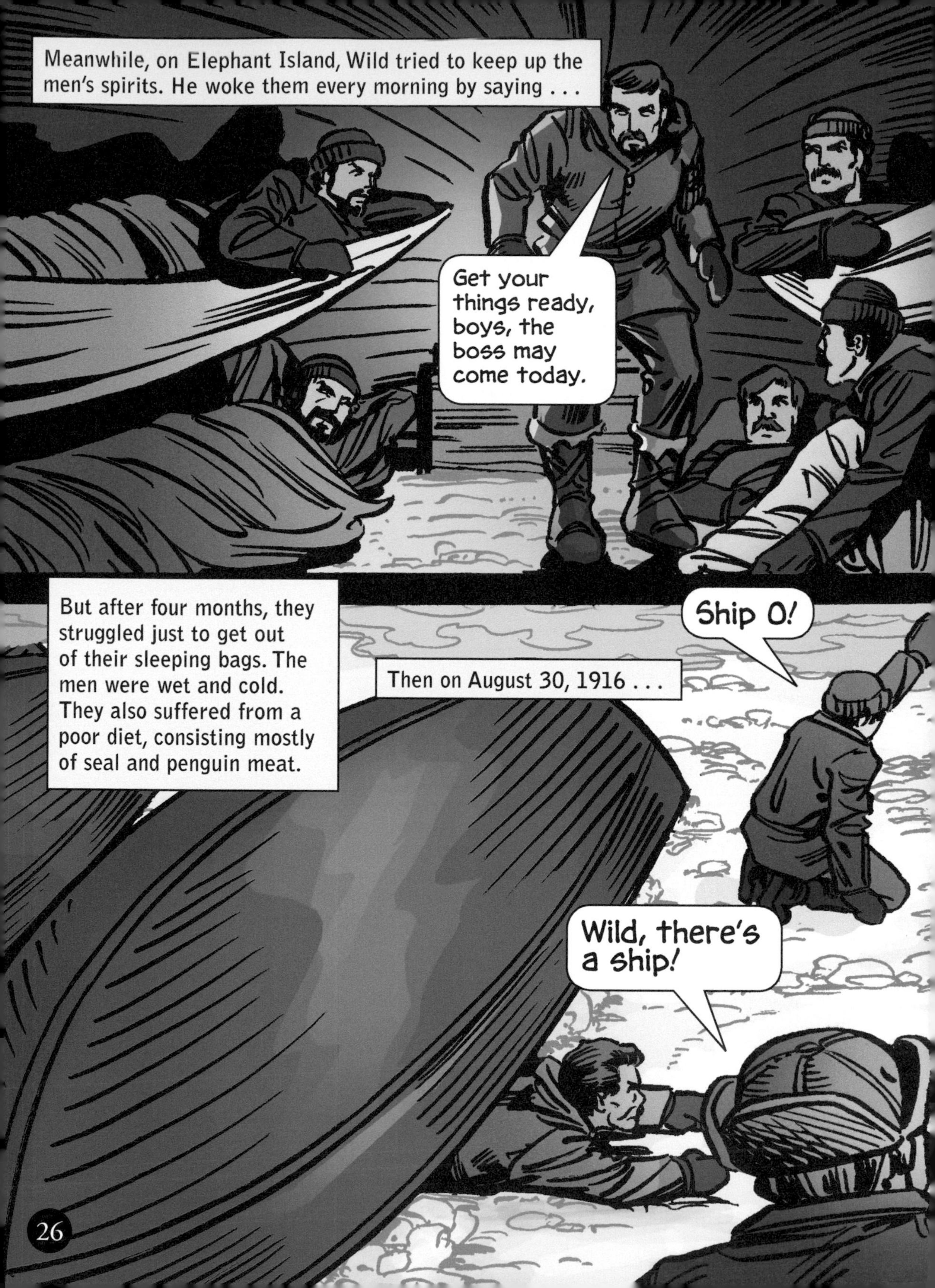
Meanwhile, on Elephant Island, Wild tried to keep up the men's spirits. He woke them every morning by saying . . .
Get your things ready, boys, the boss may come today.
But after four months, they struggled just to get out of their sleeping bags. The men were wet and cold. They also suffered from a poor diet, consisting mostly of seal and penguin meat.
Then on August 30, 1916 . . .
Ship O!
Wild, there's a ship!

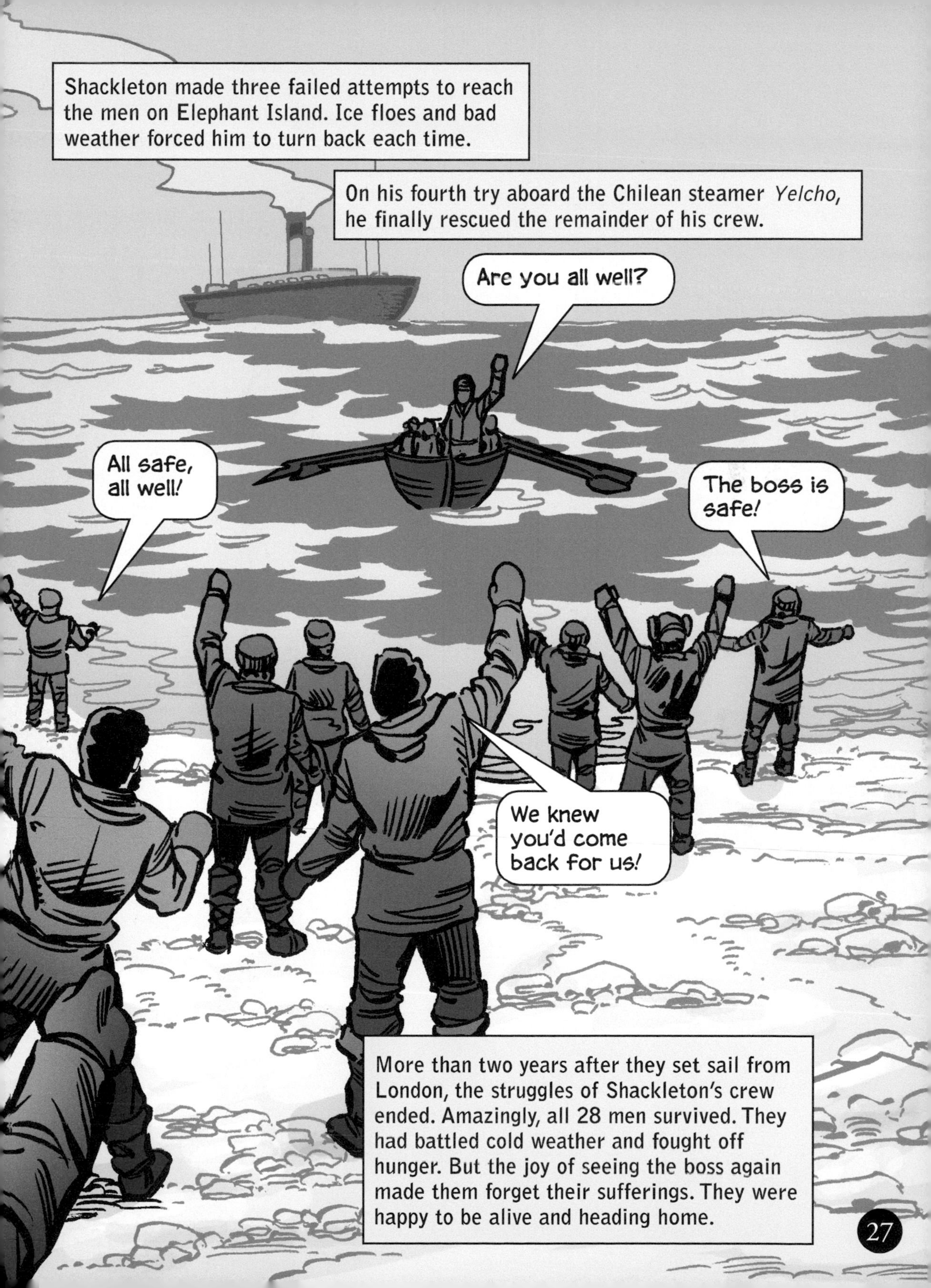
Shackleton made three failed attempts to reach the men on Elephant Island. Ice floes and bad weather forced him to turn back each time.
On his fourth try aboard the Chilean steamer *Yelcho*, he finally rescued the remainder of his crew.
Are you all well?
All safe, all well!
The boss is safe!
We knew you'd come back for us!
More than two years after they set sail from London, the struggles of Shackleton's crew ended. Amazingly, all 28 men survived. They had battled cold weather and fought off hunger. But the joy of seeing the boss again made them forget their sufferings. They were happy to be alive and heading home.

More about Ernest Shackleton

 Ernest Henry Shackleton was born February 15, 1874, in County Kildare, Ireland. His parents were Abraham and Henrietta Shackleton. Shackleton was the second of 10 children.

 In 1901, Shackleton left on his first trip to Antarctica. The National Antarctic Expedition was led by British naval officer Robert Falcon Scott. Scott and Shackleton attempted to find a way to the South Pole. They fell short of their goal by 450 miles.

 On April 9, 1904, Shackleton married Emily Dorman. They had two sons, Raymond and Edward, and one daughter, Cecily.

 In 1907, Shackleton led an expedition to reach the South Pole. He came within 97 miles of his goal. Shackleton turned back because he and his men were nearly out of supplies. Even though he failed to reach the South Pole, Shackleton was considered a hero for trying. The British king knighted him Sir Ernest Shackleton. Shackleton published a book, *The Heart of the Antarctic*, about his expedition.

In 1911, Robert Falcon Scott and Norwegian explorer Roald Amundsen led separate expeditions to reach the South Pole. Scott was not trained to use dog sleds. He and his men pulled, or "man-hauled," their sleds full of supplies. Amundsen was a skilled dog sled driver. By using dog sleds, he was able to travel twice as fast as Scott. Amundsen reached the South Pole on December 14. Scott and his companions arrived a month later. They died during their return trip from the Pole.

 In 1914, as Shackleton's expedition was about to set sail, fighting broke out in Europe. Great Britain and France went to war with Germany and Austria-Hungary. Shackleton offered the service of his ship and crew to Winston Churchill, who later became British prime minister. But Churchill told Shackleton to go on with his expedition.

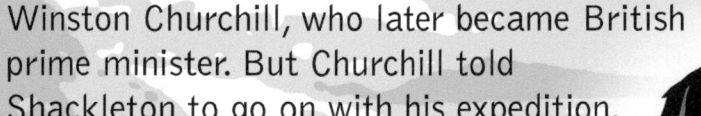

 In 1921, Shackleton left on what would be his last expedition. While staying on South Georgia, he died of heart failure January 5, 1922, at age 47. He was buried on South Georgia.

Glossary

endurance (en-DUR-uhnss)—the ability to withstand hardships

expedition (ek-spuh-DIH-shuhn)—a journey for purpose of exploration or scientific research

floe (FLOH)—a sheet of floating ice

pemmican (PEM-mi-kuhn)—a mixture of dried meat and fruit

pressure ridge (PREH-shur RIDG)—ice floes that have been upturned from the pressure of pushing against each other

Internet Sites

FactHound offers a safe, fun way to find Internet sites related to this book. All of the sites on FactHound have been researched by our staff.

Here's how:

1. *Visit www.facthound.com*
2. Type in this special code **0736854827** for age-appropriate sites. Or enter a search word related to this book for a more general search.
3. Click on the **Fetch It** button.

FactHound will fetch the best sites for you!

Read More

Calvert, Patricia. *Sir Ernest Shackleton: By Endurance We Conquer.* Great Explorations. New York: Benchmark Books, 2003.

Currie, Stephen. *Antarctica.* Exploration and Discovery. San Diego: Lucent Books, 2004.

Hooper, Meredith. *Antarctic Adventure: Exploring the Frozen South.* New York: DK, 2000.

White, Matt. *Endurance: Shipwreck and Survival on a Sea of Ice.* Mankato, Minn.: Capstone Curriculum Publishing, 2002.

Bibliography

Alexander, Caroline. *The* Endurance*: Shackleton's Legendary Antarctic Expedition.* New York: Alfred E. Knopf, 1998.

Lansing, Alfred. *Endurance: Shackleton's Incredible Voyage.* Wheaton, Ill.: Tyndale House, 1999.

Shackleton, Ernest. *South: A Memoir of the* Endurance *Voyage.* New York: Carroll & Graf, 1998.

Index